Team Spirit Speaks

Louise Hermann

Team Spirit Speaks

Copyright © 2011 Louise Hermann
All rights reserved. No part of this publication may be reproduced, stored in a retrieval system or transmitted in any form or by any means, electronic, mechanical, photocopying, recording or otherwise, without the prior written permission of the publisher.

The information, views, opinions and visuals expressed in this publication are solely those of the author(s) and do not reflect those of the publisher. The publisher disclaims any liabilities or responsibilities whatsoever for any damages, libel or liabilities arising directly or indirectly from the contents of this publication.

A copy of this publication can be found in the National Library of Australia.

ISBN: 987-1-742841-33-5 (pbk.)

Published by Book Pal
www.bookpal.com.au

Acknowledgement

On this side of life

To all of my family, friends, helpers and supporters for believing and trusting in my work.

Gratitude to my own soul for taking on this remarkable journey in this life.

On the other side

To all my deceased relatives and friends who are a constant beacon of guiding light.

A special acknowledgement of my spirit guides, friends and helpers who are known to me as *Team Spirit* and an inspiration for many souls.

I would also like to acknowledge my editor Sabina Collins and photographer Tanya Shaw. A special thank you to the proofreaders as well.

For more information on Louise, please visit *www.louisehermann.com*

Contents

Foreword

Acceptance	1
Affirmation	3
Afterlife	5
Anxiety	7
Attitude	10
Balance	12
Beauty	14
Belief	16
Caretaking	19
Celebration	21
Children	23
Communication	26
Community	28
Compassion	30
Conditions	33
Connectivity	35
Crisis	37
Cycles	39
Death	42
Direction	45
Discipline	47
Doubt	49
Dreams	51
Eclipse	54
Emotion	56
Energy	58
Experience	60
Faith	63

Family	65
Fear	67
Feelings	69
Food	71
Forgiveness	73
Freedom	76
Free Will	77
Frustration	80
Gifts	82
Giving	84
Goodbye	87
Gratitude	89
Greetings	91
Grief	94
Growth	96
Guides	98
Guilt	101
Happiness	103
Healing	105
Health	108
Home	110
Hope	112
Humanity	114
Humour	117
Hurt	119
Identity	121
Individuality	123
Innocence	126
Inspiration	128
Intention	130
Intuition	133

Jealousy	135
Joy	137
Judgement	139
Kindness	142
Knowledge	144
Leadership	146
Life Experiences	148
Listening	150
Loneliness	153
Love	155
Manifestation	156
Meditation	159
Messages	161
Mind Over Matter	164
Music	166
Nature	169
Negativity	171
Oneness	174
Outlook	176
Pain	178
Past	180
Peace	183
Possibilities	185
Power	188
Prayer	190
Purpose	192
Quality	194
Regret	196
Relationships	198
Rest	201
Sadness	203

Separation	205
Silence	207
Simplicity	210
Spirit	212
Stress	215
Surrender	217
Trust and Truth	219
Values	221
Wisdom	224
Youth	226

Foreword

This book of 100 speeches has been written in an altered channelled state with my spirit guides on the other side known as "Team Spirit" inspiring the words. The purpose of the book is to provide inspiration and guidance on how to live a more fulfilled and truthful life whilst on the earth plane. You may wish to read the book from end to end or you can open a topic on its own if the subject matter is of relevance to what you are currently experiencing in your life.

I do hope you enjoy the reading and soul growth from this book.

Acceptance

Truth is the only avenue to follow when attempting to achieve happiness in your life. Upon acceptance of this, you will begin to embrace the circumstances and people you considered to cause you grief and pain in the past. Once you know and understand that decisions and actions are not always directly aimed at you then you can attempt to see things differently – through the eyes of others.

There are reasons why certain actions are undertaken by specific people. You may never know the deeper answers of how their conclusions were reached, but you can attempt to accept that at the time of those circumstances it was considered to be their truth. This does not give justification to their initial thought patterns but merely allows you the opportunity to understand that not everyone will see things the same way in life.

Unfortunately, negative situations in your past can leave you feeling damaged and mentally exhausted. You may feel a certain anger and resentment towards those who remind you of the people who inflicted pain on you previously. If you were not able to defend yourself in the past, you are prone to overreact when faced with similar circumstances.

Even if the situation is completely different to what you have experienced before, your mind can still create a scenario that projects a reality similar to the past. A sense of paranoia can set in, causing you to think and act on an irrational basis. This is often further heightened by the use of recreational drugs, alcohol or misuse of prescribed medication.

The truth for one person can be completely different to another's truth. These polarities can result in confrontation, leaving another feeling mentally, emotionally or physically harmed. Either way, acceptance that help is required is the first step in ensuring that conflict resolution is a possibility in the future.

Sometimes it only takes one party to recognise and accept that the truth of the matter is not clearly exposed. Drilling into the underlying causes of these thoughts and actions can bring about a sense of peace for all who are observing and experiencing this behaviour. Mistrusting one another inhibits the acceptance of yourself and others.

The acceptance of "who you are" is important in understanding what life is all about. Feeling, touching and embracing your existence and the existence of others will give you the opportunity to see the horizons beyond the rocky mountains. This will give new understanding and meaning to the flow of life in troubled waters and the continuous obstacles that all souls face in their lifetime.

Once you accept that you are a powerful being incarnated onto earth for a physical existence, then you are able to embrace the possibility that there is a greater plan to your life. This roadmap requires you to identify new possibilities and opportunities when they arise in the hope that you will surrender. The trust in yourself and the universe requires you to believe in "who you are" through many levels of life experience.

Affirmation

The human mind can build belief systems that certain experiences in life are not worthy of their soul. Many people seek outside approval to obtain positive feedback that specific outcomes are possibilities within their lifetime. These sources of influence can be given by themselves or other human beings through inspirations provided in audio or visual means.

You do not need permission to give to yourself the gifts of life. You do not need to continuously self-examine and self-criticise to the point until you reach the conclusion that you are a well-deserving human being. Your soul has the opportunity to experience the wonders and adventures of exploring "who you are" in many different ways every day.

Confirmation that you are a part of something far greater than yourself is already known in each of you. A true affirmation is one that opens your heart and mind to possibilities that were never before imagined. This is not the grandest physical creation of all outcomes but rather a simple reminder that you are of spirit and the limitations placed on you are attributes of the earth plane and not your soul.

If you were to accept that nothing can ever harm you and the physical world is a transitory place for your current existence, then you would appreciate your experiences right here in the now. You would understand that true affirmation is the gratitude you feel for being alive with all those you care so dearly for. You would know that you are never alone, as those who have moved to the next life will always be watching and guiding you.

Confirmation of "who you are" cannot be experienced outside of yourself. It is the embracing of the various aspects of yourself and others in the hope that you will recognise a part of you that has remained dormant throughout your life so far. It is self-acceptance and self-love without judgement or criticism. It is the approval of the life you are currently living and truly deserve.

If you wish to provide yourself with positive affirmations on a daily basis then continue to do so. This is healthy for the mind, body and spirit by resonating higher vibrations of hope and trust in humanity and the universe. It will assist you in the manifestations of your dreams and bring about a sense of reality that is aligned with your soul purpose and journey.

It is also important to observe the negative affirmations you send to yourself each day. Just as you choose to entertain the positive thought patterns in your mind, you can also take the option to ignore and finally remove the opinions you may have placed on yourself or others that are negative in nature.

So much energy is wasted in the minds of many by inflicting self-pain and self-harm onto their physical world reality. Very little room can be created for positive affirmations if you choose to entertain that you are worthless and not deserving of a happy and healthy life. When these thoughts arise in your mind, recognise them immediately and tell yourself you are a beautiful and radiant human being. From this, you will soon realise that life can be joyful and wonderful for all who wish to experience it.

Afterlife

When you think of the afterlife, your thoughts will vary considerably based on your own beliefs and values. If you believe that another place exists where life will continue beyond physical death, then this will be the situation for you. If you believe that there is no life after leaving this world, you may find yourself in a surprising situation upon passing to the other side.

Many people speak of the possibilities of what life will be like when departing the earth plane. Will they continue to experience joy, happiness and recognition of loved ones who may have gone before them? Will they be able to communicate with those on this side of life even though they no longer have a physical body?

Just as life on the earth plane differs from continent to continent and country to country, so too does life in the spirit world. Each and every place will have its own unique characteristics and every one of you will contribute to the surrounding environment just like you do in your current existence. Souls will have a place of residence that you may refer to as a home where your spirit can rest and enjoy life.

Upon the initial process of physical death, you will find yourself in an atmosphere that is suited to your recent emotional and mental mindset. Helpers from the spirit world will be at hand to provide you with various forms of healing and your loved ones and friends on the other side will be waiting for your arrival. There will be an overwhelming sense of love throughout your ethereal body once you enter the world of light.

Depending on the mental state of your passing, you will require some adjustments in your way of thinking in a world that is no longer physical. You may choose to continue certain activities that you enjoyed here on earth until you realise that these are either no longer necessary or greater possibilities are at hand for you. Encouragement is always given to souls entering their new life, with like minds attracting one another for company and healing.

Time and space as you know it here in the physical world will differ considerably. You will not be confined to thinking that you are limited to only one place at a time. You can move around to visit various places and see different people, resulting in experiencing simultaneous events. You can travel to different parts of the earth plane and universe, depending on your own thoughts and desires.

The physical body that you know today, which is ageing and becoming less vibrant throughout time, will be superseded by your ethereal body, which is a replica of your earthly body in its healthiest state. You will no longer be affected by the mental or physical illnesses that exist on earth and love and support will be given to you on an emotional wellbeing level.

You will no longer have worries about money, food, shelter and clothing, as your body will be operating at a non-physical-matter vibration. Your status in society will not be ranked by order of wealth, education or hierarchical structure, but rather your attraction will be of light and the love that you project to yourself and others. This is why it is important that you discover and embrace "who you are" and connect with others prior to physical death.

Anxiety

When you are feeling worried or anxious about something, it means you are unsure about the outcome of a future event or circumstance. It may have been past situations that contributed to those feelings, but ultimately you are unable to enjoy the present due to those thoughts arising in your mind.

Even though you attempt to tell yourself you are going to be alright, there can be continued challenges in quietening the mind.

At times of uncertainty in your life, always attempt to visualise the happiest moments you have experienced. Close your eyes for just a few moments and take yourself to a place where you have felt comfortable and loved. Ask yourself what parts of you were fulfilled in those moments and what, where and who were the contributing factors to those blissful times.

Once you are able to remember that life was not always difficult or challenging, your mind can then wander to those times of joy and happiness in the hope that you will temporarily escape the worries you're currently facing. Do not be embarrassed about your feelings and emotions but rather embrace them to be a part of "who you are" along the road of self-discovery in this current physical lifetime.

Once you begin to share your own hurt and pain, then others can be inspired to do the same. You may find that those you have attracted into your life have similar circumstances to you but may not have previously expressed it openly and honestly. At a deeper soul level you naturally connected to one another in the hope that healing and love could be shared and experienced together.

In a world that is dominated by media of fear, violence and rejection, it is important that you maintain a balance on what you receive and perceive into your own reality. If you are constantly subjecting yourself to negative thoughts and actions, you may begin to believe that this is how everyone thinks and behaves. This can then greatly affect your interaction with other human beings.

It is more common for the human mind to input energy into the negative rather than positive thoughts of life. Through lack of self-love and judgement of yourself and others, this can provide you with an excuse not to progress further into knowing "who you are". Your beliefs may tell you that others are holding you back. However, it is only when you embrace "who you are" that others will not affect your reality.

Through the universal laws of free will and choice, the power to create a wonderful and fulfilling life is in your hands. Certain circumstances and events have been chosen in your current life to provide you with an opportunity to expand "who you are" at the soul level.

Happiness and self-fulfilment is not provided through material wealth. Worrying about the finances of tomorrow will not give you a sense of security and power around you. Attempting to control the actions and thoughts of those you care deeply for will not provide you with joy or pleasure. This will only provide you with further worry and stress. Embrace your own life and in time you will realise that your happiness will stem from enjoying the present moments that have been given to you.

Attitude

Attitude in your life has an effect on everything you say and do. If you do not believe in what you say then your actions will clearly reflect this. You may not be aware of this consciously but at the soul level you will know the difference. In order to express "who you are" you need to be true to yourself, which includes monitoring your own attitude towards life.

If you find yourself in the company of those who hold a positive attitude then this will consciously and unconsciously influence your own decision-making processes. A mindset of creation and expansion can inspire people on many levels, allowing them to express aspects of "who they are". This will provide them with a reminder that all of humanity is connected on a deeper soul level.

The wanting of others to succeed and be happy in life is a healthy attitude that should be shared by all. Feelings of envy and jealousy are not warranted in a life that hopes to be fulfilled with love and joy. The knowingness that everyone has the right to be cared for by others should be embraced by humanity at large.

Supporting one another through spirituality, finances, education and physical needs is required in order to understand the true meaning of a positive attitude. When your mind is clear of negative thoughts and self-indulgence, you are able to reflect on the progression of your own thoughts and actions as well as those around you.

Never believe that your thoughts and actions are static. You are an ever-changing soul who has the ability to create a shift in attitude at will. It is your choice how you wish to perceive yourself, the world and others. Life is dynamic and so is your spirit in expressing itself through life experiences of both challenging and rewarding behaviour.

Admiration for others who have a positive attitude is not enough to cause a shift. You need to believe that you are worthy of such a mindset and capable of executing the new thoughts into your current reality. The removal of a more negative dense mindset will take practise and time. It can also be greatly influenced by those who love and care for you on a day-to-day basis.

If you wish to view life in a more positive manner, express this openly to those around you. Do not ask for approval or permission but simply let others know that you no longer wish to entertain energy that is non-productive to your life. Give them a few examples of how this has contributed to your setbacks in the past and they may extend themselves further to you through compassion.

If you feel that a lack of understanding in sharing your new thoughts and actions may be experienced, then you may decide to keep this closer to your heart. Despite the gradual changes in you, continue to send loving and healing thoughts to others and they will receive these unconsciously. Over time you may be surprised to find that their mindset will also change, without them even being aware of the source of inspiration.

Balance

When you are feeling rushed or not "in the moment" of life, then it is important that you take a deep breath and examine your circumstances. Life was not meant to be a chore executed on a day-to-day basis but rather an experience filled with pleasure, joy, happiness and love, as well as other lessons of pain and heartache.

Achieving balance in your life is not easy. To stand at any one point in time and say that all is balanced within and around you would be unrealistic. Your perspective of balance will differ greatly to others but it is your response to the circumstances that will make the difference.

If you encourage others to find calm and peace within themselves, then this should also make you happy regardless of the choices they have made. Acceptance of "who you are" and the encouraging of souls in your life involves the embracing of the lifestyles they may wish to engage in. If their free will and choice does not inflict hurt and pain onto themselves or others then there is no reason why this should affect anyone else.

It is only when you attempt to control the lives of others that large imbalances can be felt. Wanting other souls to agree with your terms and conditions or way of life can be very disappointing for you, given that most of the time they will not listen anyway. Even a child who is instructed to think or act under certain conditions will rebel and become resentful in time.

If you attempt to encourage souls to shine and be the best person they can be, then the result can be somewhat different. Allow the individual to expand and accept "who they are" on many levels and from this your participation will provide further reflection and balance within your own life. Do not measure success by what one has said or done. Simply embrace the moments as being times of rejoicing.

If someone has acted out to you in a manner that has caused you hurt and pain then share this experience with them. Do not hold onto the thoughts and actions in the hope that the pain will simply go away without attending to the matter. You can choose to either do this unconsciously by sending them love, light and forgiveness or you can decide to share this consciously through further discussion.

Always allow yourself the opportunity to re-examine any circumstance or situation once the emotion has settled down. You may see through clarity that a misunderstanding has occurred or perhaps judgements were made based on beliefs or past experiences. Understanding the human mind is difficult and attempting to control or manipulate thoughts will cause further imbalances.

Accept that you are a spirit being experiencing life through a physical world. You always have the choice to rise above a situation from a spiritual perspective in the attempt to grow and understand. Once you know and embrace this concept in your own mind, you can then inspire yourself and others to become an instrument of peace and love for all of humanity to share.

Beauty

Whenever you take the time to look into the mirror, ask yourself, "who is this person?". Extend your focus into your eyes and allow your mind to drift into a relaxed state. Over time you will discover that the external physical body becomes less of a focal point and more of a shadow, faded into the distant background. You will soon be comfortable examining yourself without judgement.

The physical body is made up of matter that serves a purpose for you to have an experience on the earth plane. It allows you to enjoy the wonders of life through thoughts, feelings, emotions, touch and movement. There are times when your body may not operate at its full capacity, which can cause you to concentrate on function rather than beauty.

Generally when a person is young, a lot of energy is placed into their physical appearance. They may like to impress others with fashion, fitness, makeup and exposure in the hope that they will discover "who they are". Acceptance from peers and even strangers can bring about a yearning to be included into the normality of the society they live in.

Being of youth carries a beauty within itself. At a time when the mind, body and spirit is more naive and untouched there can be less appreciation than otherwise would be expected. Young people tend to be more carefree than the older population and can be inspired to operate spontaneously most of the time.

Your body can carry less physical scars and wounds in your earlier years. However, throughout these years when your body is at its peak you can also easily open yourself to self-criticism and judgement. You may have hoped to be thinner, taller, faster, larger or darker, which creates a lack of worth and scars or wounds within your own mind.

The human experience can bypass the phases of gratitude until something is completely gone. Once the physical body changes through injury or ill-health, there can be a sudden shift in mindset that previously may not have existed. You may no longer be concerned with the aesthetic side of your body but rather its ability to operate successfully on a day-to-day basis.

It should not take the loss of youth, health or function for you to appreciate the vessel you currently reside in. Beauty in the physical sense is only skin deep and is ever-changing as your environment and lifestyle shifts. For something that is so temporary in your experience, a lot of energy is placed on its appearance.

If the population accepted and knew that they were much more than a physical body, they would see their bodies quite differently. Instead of investing so much time and effort on self-indulgence, cosmetic surgery or fashion they would concentrate more on sustaining a fit and healthy lifestyle in the hope of achieving fulfilling experiences of soul growth and awareness.

Meditation, prayer and alternative methods of healing would be investigated as they began to understand that the mind, body and spirit are all connected. A soul's beauty in the spirit world is identified through the brightness of the love and light that shines from their energy field. If you accept and activate "who you are" in this lifetime, your beauty will be far greater than you could ever have imagined here on the earth plane in a human physical body.

Belief

Throughout your life there will be times when your belief system will alter greatly. This can be the result of your own experiences or witnessing others change into much happier and fulfilled people. Regardless of your current or past foundations, it does not matter what you believe in as long as it inspires your spirit and others.

There are so many different belief systems on how to live a life on the earth plane which has brought about diversity in spirituality. Some believe that they must personally suffer in this life in order to experience joy in the afterlife. Others believe the opposite, whereby the torture and killing of souls in the physical world will bring about rewards and fulfilment upon death.

When making decisions based on core belief systems, use common sense in your approach to selecting the delivery method of faith. Attempt to bring about a balance in your own energy and its delivery to others. Ask yourself, in terms of morals and values, what is important to you in this life and try to execute a lifestyle that coincides with them.

If you see the earth plane as a wonderful place of residence that has been given for all to enjoy then you should also view the same for yourself. The planet needs to be nurtured and taken care of, just like your physical body does. If it is polluted, then the minds that reside within its habitat need to take some form of ownership for the contamination and loss of purity. The same also exists for the alignment of your own mind, body and spirit in this lifetime.

When something occurs in life that is unexpected or unwanted, it is much easier to blame an outside universal force than attempt to look within. This force can be another soul in your life or a higher being that you may refer to as God. Either way, in times of adversity the first most common place to ask for help is outside of oneself. There can be a lack of belief that you are a powerful being in control of your thoughts and actions within your own existence.

Do not disconnect from others who may differ greatly to your belief systems. If they live a life of similar morals and values to you, the only variances may be in their method of faith. Every human being has their own way of expressing "who they are". Some may not express it openly through words but rather practise their giving through actions instead.

A healthy belief system is one that encourages an open mind and open heart. As the human race changes and evolves over time, so too should the knowledge and understanding of life and connectivity. If someone provides you with wisdom that holds true to "who you are"; do not attempt to dissect it.

Take any new form of wisdom which promotes self-love, acceptance, lack of judgement and oneness as a gift given from one soul to another. Attempt to see the goodness in yourself and your fellow human beings. Focus on the similarities instead of the differences. You are all of spirit and no spirit should ever be denied the opportunity to experience joy, love, truth and happiness in their lifetime.

Caretaking

Taking care of someone in the spirit world seems to be a topic of interest amongst many people. Most people know that their loved ones are taken care of either by deceased relatives and friends, angelic beings of light, the divine and other helpers to make the transition process easier. All human beings know at a soul level that transition from one world to another is done with assistance and love.

If transition from one world to another is done through compassion and understanding, then why is this knowingness not applied to everyday life on the earth plane? Why do you need to wait until physical death to believe that love and support is around you? Why are you not currently worthy of such assistance and love from human beings on your own plane of existence?

Many assume that love and caretaking needs to be done by angels. Why can't you be an angel or helper for others in need? The physical world is much harder to live in than the spirit world so there is a greater need for this type of assistance on this side of the veil. Assistance through a living person is always required to assist in the help required on the earth plane.

Caretaking requires taking care of yourself as well as your fellow human beings. Taking care of the mind, body and spirit is of importance. These three parts of yourself do exist and from this acknowledgement you can then identify the needs in others. If you are not able to physically assist someone financially, this does not mean that you cannot assist them by providing a positive mindset or igniting their spirit.

In today's society, many believe that caretaking is a role that is undertaken through the form of duty. If you work as a nurse, volunteer or teacher then you are viewed as an automatic caretaker. But should this hat be worn only whilst working in these roles? Can others who do not formally undertake these types of work also assist humanity? Hats can be moulded in many different shapes and sizes and for most human beings, one size does fit all.

Your ability to help people each and every day is right in front of you. The ability for others to assist in your own lives is there as well. Make your presence known as every human being is not always aware of the needs and intentions of people around them. Voice your needs and your intentions to assist. It is only when you voice this that your actions can then speak louder than words.

Do not be afraid of judgement when asking for help. Do you ask for assistance from the spirit world because you know you will not be judged? Perhaps through your actions you can teach others not to judge by setting an example. By naturally opening your heart to both giving and receiving, you will find that many people on the earth plane can be caretakers for themselves and each other.

Celebration

When you embrace your current life as a wonderful gift, you will then be able to give gratitude to your own existence. Life is meant to be enjoyable and it is important that you include celebration in your day-to-day lives. This does not mean that you need to continually host parties or attend them, instead simply stop and enjoy the finer things in life such as smelling the flowers in the garden.

It is through physical death that most souls come to view their lives so differently. The gifts of taste and smell may have been taken for granted throughout their earthly lives. The ability to touch another soul in physical form or the wonderful plants and animals that exist on the planet are celebrations throughout your life that do not cost any money. This type of energy exchange can be very fulfilling for your mind, body and spirit.

If you observe those around you who seem to be truly happy in their lives, you will see a pattern of simplicity. Even though some may be fortunate in material wealth, their approach to kindness and love is one that can be felt in their presence. The welcoming feelings they project to you will be similar to the embracing of their own soul and "who they are".

It is important that you do not place a direct correlation between physical world material gain and unhappiness. It is not the objects themselves that create misery amongst the people but rather the ego and judgement through separation that cause most of the problems. There are people in positions of power and wealth who see their gifts as a celebration that must be shared with those who are less fortunate.

One of the greatest tests a soul can be given is to be offered the world and then give some of it away. True character can be seen when a person who has worked hard towards self-empowerment and self-acceptance makes decisions that ultimately benefit the greater consciousness. Instead of projecting jealous thoughts and resentment towards these souls, attempt to celebrate their kindness to others.

Celebrating your life and the lives of others is important in the process of discovering "who you are". There are times in your life when certain souls will inflict hurt and pain onto you, either intentionally or they may be completely unaware of their thoughts or actions. Throughout those times you can decide if you wish to embrace the gifts and greater learning from the exchange, or become a victim of circumstance.

It does not matter how difficult things may become or how terrible someone is to you, never allow the light within "who you are" to dim. Stay true to yourself and know that you are a potential teacher for many people who cannot find their way through life. You can ultimately guide yourself and others who may be influenced by belief systems that promote lack of self-love and self-worth.

It is through adversity that your human spirit discovers "who you are". It is only when your ego has been tested that you can see the potential darkness that can stem from yourself at times of crisis. Make decisions in these moments that allow you to rise above the low-level vibrations of anger, fear, jealousy, hatred and resentment. Know that you are much more than this and celebrate the essence of your own spirit through forgiveness, love, joy, happiness, truth, kindness and hope.

Children

Children are viewed as the flame or source of life. When there is a loss of a child on this side of life, there seems to be a greater level of grief for those left behind. But is it the grief of the loss of your own inner child that is of equal importance throughout this challenging time?

It is questionable as to what is lost when a child moves on from its physical form on the earth plane. Is it the loss of innocence that the child expresses? Or is it the pureness and naivety of one's soul? It is a combination of these attributes that makes the loss so unbearable. So how did these adult souls manage before the child spirits came into their lives? They too were once carefree and ever so giving without judgement.

A child is a reminder of "who you are" and children truly believe that the impossible can be achieved.

They affect many people around them, even strangers who walk on the street. A smile, wave or a silly giggle will move any soul, no matter how difficult life may be. It is this loss, the void in one's inner peace that is the greatest loss of harmony and joy on earth.

A child does not know the difference between the various religions, races or lifestyle choices one can make. Children will assimilate these thoughts from adults and even create their own interpretation of these choices at a much higher level. You may find them drawing a black Jesus, a family unit comprising two dads and three mums, or even identifying the dog as a major family player in a household environment.

For children, life is not a chore or a way to exist on a day-to-day basis, but rather an adventure that seems to have no ending. It is this no-ending, no concept of time and space that allows them to capture a spiritual experience right here on earth. The spirit world is one of thought and imagination is the basis of creativity. Children are natural creators of their own reality and by observing their behaviour you will have a clearer idea of how your loved ones live in the spirit world.

In a mental world, your loved ones who wanted to be artists, musicians or architects can do so without the physical limitations they may have experienced here on earth. Limitations are not placed on the earth plane as a force in its magnetic field, rather they are thoughts you have placed on each other. The inability to identify what your thoughts are, as well as the creation of expectations, are the first stages of closing down this aspect of your own child spirit within.

Children do not understand that there is not enough energy to go around. They are natural creators and truly believe that more can be created for the underprivileged. The earth can sufficiently provide enough food and clothing for all its inhabitants but it is the belief system of the adults that is limiting. Everyone can come together to create and therefore provide a more equal share for all souls on earth.

The loss of a child at a young age on earth does not just cause grief owing to the fact that their life span was short and certain milestones were not achieved. It is much more than that. It is the loss of the reminder of what life is all about and what can be achieved through imagination in creating one's own reality.

When a child moves from this world to the spirit world, very little will change in their reality. Their transition will be easier than for adults as their imagination and creativity will continue to blossom in a world that will accept all thoughts as real. Children will not be told to close down their imagination that such beautiful things do not exist, for they will exist for all children and adults if it be their request.

The next time you think of a child who may have crossed over to the spirit world, think of them in an atmosphere that is more suited to their own mental reality that could not be fulfilled on earth. If you are an adult who has simply lost your way, then take the pleasure to sit and observe the children. They will naturally take you on a journey through the loss of time and space that will allow you to expand your own wings of imagination and create the life you truly deserve.

Communication

The ability to communicate effectively, openly and honestly with one another is perhaps one of the greatest set of skills you can acquire in your lifetime. By removing the barriers of thought that can exist between assumptions and judgements, you are able to express yourself in the hope that others will both understand and embrace your way of thinking.

By speaking truthfully on how you feel about something, you always carry the possibility of touching another person's soul with honesty. If the delivery of your words is done through compassion and love, your effect on the greater consciousness of humanity can be far greater again. If you can control the need to express that you are right and others are wrong, a level playing field can then be established for all to express "who they are".

Communication can be done in ways that do not require words. A smile to a person walking on the street or a gentle wave can provide someone with feelings of hope and happiness, even if you don't know them. Their soul connects with your spirit in the hope that the rest of the day will be more enjoyable through your energy exchange.

Embracing one another through hugs and kisses can provide your mind, body and spirit with fulfilment, especially in challenging times of life. Placing your arms around someone who feels alone or abandoned can give them a sense of security that words could otherwise not provide. The human touch can be a pleasant way to communicate with one another in physical form.

You do not need to be a great public speaker or writer in order to communicate effectively. Ensuring that you are connecting through words that others will understand and feel inspired by is of importance. Attempting to place fear and intimidation into the vocabulary will only result in a withdrawal of attention and lack of self-worth and self-confidence for those absorbing the input.

The use of writing through poetry and novels can be a wonderful avenue to open the soul. It allows the author to provide a viewpoint of life without having to personally engage in the physical attributes and expressions of speaking. It can leave the reader impacted through feelings of inner peace and joy.

Positive communication should leave the soul feeling elated about the experience. Their energy can shift in a way that allows them to open their hearts and minds to new learning and possibilities that otherwise may have remained dormant in the discovery path of "who they are". The use of humour and fun is healthy for the spirit, which can then encourage aspects of personalities to come forward and celebrate.

By expressing yourself to others in an open and honest manner, you will find that you will begin to enjoy your own company more. Communication with yourself in a silent and subtle nature can provide you with a foundation in supporting your current thoughts and actions. You can then enjoy accepting your own soul in a way that provides you with comfort and security that will be with you at all times.

Community

Feelings of being part of something far greater than yourself can provide a foundation of knowing that you are all connected on a deeper soul level. The best place to recognise this is to be part of a community. Every person can play a different role which can leave feelings of gratitude amongst each other at times.

If you feel at times that you are not understood or heard by your close family or friends, attempt to extend yourself to others of like-minded thoughts in different places within your society. You do not need to be part of an association or group to meet other people but rather open your heart and mind to new possibilities of friendships and companions in your life.

These newly formed relationships may only last for short periods of time in the physical world but the soul imprint in your consciousness can be long-lasting. Someone can inspire or motivate you in such a way that an instant connection can be felt. You may wish to assist others in the growth or teaching of "who they are" so that hope and faith can be restored into their lives.

When communicating and interacting with other souls, there is no need to attempt to define what the outcome will be. True bonding between your spirits occurs naturally through the wonders of friendship, joy, humour and love. You will often find that an initial connection with someone can lead you into a stronger relationship with another person through introduction.

Interacting with the plants and animals that surround your community is also very important. Appreciating the trees that provide you with oxygen in your daily lives allows you to give thanks to your current existence on the planet. This can encourage a greater level of respect for a cleaner and safer environment for the earth as a whole.

Walking through community gardens and parks are wonderful ways to enjoy the outdoors. You will meet and greet people who are connected to the beauty of the flowers and the protection of the trees. Children and animals can lift the atmosphere, giving hope and happiness to those who are privileged enough to be present.

If you wish to raise your children in a place that is trusting, then be more open and honest with those who surround your environment. By setting an example of peace and oneness you may inspire others to do the same, which can result in less crime and violence in your society. This can then lead to community programs that will encourage working together rather than against one another.

It is natural for human beings to make eye contact with people they consider to be strangers. There may not be a smile that follows the initial connection, but some form of recognition does occur. This can then be overshadowed by thoughts of judgement, or you can simply choose to acknowledge that the person is a soul living on earth just like yourself.

Always remember that the more disconnected you become from your family, friends and community at large, the less energy you will have to embrace the wonders of life. Every person has an exchange of energy to offer another soul, regardless of how light or dark their circumstances may seem. Accepting that you are part of a society can be very rewarding for those who are willing to engage in the discovery of "who they are".

Compassion

There are times in your life where you will feel the need to reach out to others in an attempt to provide comfort in some way. This wanting to assist those who may be less fortunate than yourself is a natural part of "who you are". Being connected to souls outside your routine life is healthy for anyone wishing to pursue the journey of self-discovery.

It is through reaching out to people who are in need that you can begin to see the gratitude in your own lives. By observing a soul struggling with pain, illness, grief, loneliness, sadness or fear, you will soon realise that the support you have around you and within you is a wonderful part of your existence. By observing feelings of desperation and despair, you have the opportunity to assist others wherever possible throughout your experiences.

You do not need to be financially secure to reach out to anyone in need. A lot of support can be provided through listening, laughter, counselling and being present in someone else's company. The knowing that another human being cares and wishes to help in their own little way can fill one's heart with enough hope and happiness to last a long time.

Everyone has the opportunity to be an instrument of peace to many souls who require comfort. True compassion does not involve judgement or wanting to control another person. It is purely from the heart, with fulfilment felt by all parties involved in the energy exchange. This can quickly shift an atmosphere of doom and gloom to one of hope and clarity for those who are willing to surrender to assistance.

It is often asked of the spirit world to provide guidance in many different ways. What is not realised is that help has been sent on many occasions but not recognised by those who requested the assistance. If you place in your mind that specific instructions need to be followed in order for the spirit world to help you, this can greatly limit their ability to provide guidance directly to you.

The reason for this is that there may be many players who need to be involved to provide you with the most favourable outcome. You may not be able to recognise this immediately, but through trust and surrender you will feel drawn towards those signals. Once certain actions are executed then the next stage will become more evident over time.

It is important that you provide compassion to yourself and others. Understanding your own needs and wants is just as important as the guidance you give and receive. Attending to your physical-world existence requires a positive outlook with what is needed to sustain a happy and healthy life. Once you have obtained a balance in this, you can then choose to share your excess with others.

If you find that your clothing is no longer of use, take the time to cleanse them with love in the hope that they will find their way to another soul in need. Objects that can provide hours of activity or entertainment can be given to those who you feel will appreciate the gift. If you have spare time throughout your day, you may wish to volunteer amongst your community with those who will treasure your company.

Conditions

Through expectations and belief systems, the human mind can place conditions on how and when it can experience happiness and joy in its life. If you feel pressured, limited or smothered, ask yourself what conditions have been placed on your experiences. You should be able to act carefree at will without the stress and worry of what you will think of yourself afterwards or the responses of people around you.

Conditions in life can vary across a wide spectrum of religious, financial, sexual, cultural or racial expectations. If you feel the need to express yourself based on the morals and values set out in your society, over time this can create a level of resentment at a deeper soul level within "who you are".

Any condition placed on the experience of your soul does not express complete truth in "who you are". These conditions have been created by souls who believe that their truth is superior and more correct than your truth. They do not understand that society is connected on many levels and every person has the right to express "who they are" without judgement or punishment.

In a society where those in power feel the need to control the population, certain rules and regulations are created so people will adhere to their way of life. This will allow them to feel important in "who they are" so they can have the ability to say and act in a manner that may not be subjected to the conditions placed on the rest of the population.

Certain rules and regulations will need to be applied to a physical world society to ensure that resources and energy are directed towards an equitable distribution. However in many instances, this result is not the case. Income and taxes taken from the more financially secure people are not always directed towards those who require true assistance.

In terms of crime and punishment, the population needs to be educated in a pro-active manner on the consequences of harming another soul. These consequences extend beyond the mental, emotional and physical turmoil. No organisation such as a prison or an institution governed by certain spiritual beliefs can take away the actions that one soul has done to another or Karma as you may know it.

If the population was educated on unconditional love, then a controlling society governed by complex conditions would no longer be necessary. Every person would have an understanding that their compassion is shared through the love of others and the infliction of pain onto someone else only eventuates into self-harm. Once this is known and understood, then a conditioned life is no longer necessary.

Experiencing and living through unconditional love for yourself and others is very powerful. It allows you to activate parts of "who you are" in a way that breaks down all barriers within your own psyche. You can inspire others to live a carefree life in the hope that they understand and see their own light too. Always remember that unconditional love does not have limits and once this is known and expressed then your life will be greatly fulfilled with wonderful experiences.

Connectivity

When you engage in conversation with others you are connecting on many levels between the mind, body and spirit. You know they can understand you regardless of which language the words are from, as the soul and physical body language will represent "who they are". If they are of a loving and caring nature you will feel this resonate through your body as calmness embracing your spirit.

All life in the physical world and planes of existences beyond the earth are connected through energy. It is difficult for your mind to comprehend this as your reality is predominately determined by your senses of seeing and hearing. If this force is not witnessed through your normal everyday lives then it is easy to forget this greater oneness within and around you.

If you are a believer in the afterlife and can grasp the concept of an instrument connecting with your loved ones, then you have begun to open your minds to further possibilities of life. You know that the physical body is a dress code for existence within this world so you can experience an alternate reality. You have never been and never will be separated from the source of light that represents "who you are".

The light that resides in you is a beautiful beacon that should be recognised by all. It is something that needs to be embraced in your experiences in the hope that you can activate wonderful aspects of your personality in this life. Each and every one of you has gifts to present to yourselves and each other. Take these gifts and allow "who you are" to shine as far as your light will expand.

It is only through connectivity that you can truly understand "who you are". The greatest learning in life often comes through the most confronting and painful experiences with others. To receive love and then have the feelings of it being taken away from you is something that most human beings struggle to come to terms with.

You can never experience life alone. You cannot know and understand "who you are" without the interaction of other souls. Separation and disconnection does not provide you with the foundations of self-love and self-acceptance. In order to operate in an existence that is naturally connected with energy, you need to be in the flow of life and oneness of it all.

If someone has disappointed and hurt you in the past, ask yourself what the gifts of learning were for you. Did you grow in "who you are" and begin to embrace a strength that otherwise may have remained dormant in this life? Were you able to share your experience with others in the hope that it would provide them with peace and inspiration in moving forward?

If you give yourself enough love, you will come to the realisation that you deserve a happy and healthy life. Do not rely on others to give this to you. When you have excess energy, attempt to send this out to those in need. From this you will know and understand that thoughts and actions of pure nature will produce more and more positive energy, which in turn will affect the greater consciousness and connectivity of all of humanity.

Crisis

Many people consider challenging times to be a crisis in life. Sometimes these moments carry an essence of silence that allows you to discover "who you are". At times when you are forced to reassess what is of greater importance then you can seek those parts of yourself that have remained unrecognised for so long.

When one considers themselves to be subjected to continuous bad luck and misfortune then this belief system will produce the resulting outcomes as requested. If your mindset is one of doom and gloom then you can attract these situations or circumstances into your lives. Of course certain events need to occur as part of your own life path, but not all adversity you face is required on a day-to-day basis.

It is through adversity that you have the opportunity to grow. You are reminded of your strengths and weaknesses and in time these can be nurtured in a loving and caring way. Once you recognise that life on the earth plane is not meant to always be smooth, you will embrace the potential learning in all possibilities given at any point in time.

Throughout these times of challenging thoughts and actions, attempt to see the light and wonders of the greater plan at hand. Ask yourself the question that if major past events had not occurred in your life, would you be where you are today? It is through major changes that you have the opportunity to re-create yourself and move on to a new course of learning.

Often when a person faces any form of adversity, this can then flow into other areas of their life. When a death occurs in the family, it can trigger underlying emotions to take immediate action on their own personal and work relationships. Detachment of materialism can occur to the extent where the person changes their physical environment and their lifestyle.

When at least one part of the mind, body or spirit has been severely imbalanced with negative energy, then a person can consider themselves to be acting in a "crisis mode". This mode of thinking and acting can lead to irrational thoughts and behaviour causing concern for those observing the changes in emotions of the individual.

It is important that you respect yourself and others going through these challenges to ensure that your expectations do not influence the outcome. Certain catalysts of change are required in order for deeper soul level healing to occur. Self reflection for the soul can be healthy if you know that self-harm is not a risk.

Human beings tend to blame themselves or "God" throughout times of crisis. On a few occasions they give gratitude to themselves and the universe when life is running smoothly. It is this forgetting of how good life is that can create a mindset of crisis mode when times are less favourable. It seems that the pendulum moves very quickly in their mind causing emotions and feelings of being out of control.

Always remember that there is someone you can reach out to in times of desperation and need. There are many souls sent to the earth plane to heal and embrace those who find that life is harsh even on the best of days. You are never alone, for the connectivity and love amongst the human race is ever-growing.

Cycles

Life carries many forms of cycles. The seasons of summer, autumn, winter and spring all represent different aspects of what the earth has to offer in a physical existence. These extremities in conditions are an example that within a cycle there are other degrees of cycles. This can change dramatically when one factor is adjusted in the flow of life.

When a child is born into the physical world, it is similar to the spring season. The gathering of nutrition in the form of pollen is done by busy worker bees, dedicated to the role of providing new life as parents are to their child. The energy throughout the spring cycle is vibrant and new with freshness in the air that is contagious to those observing and experiencing it.

As the child grows into an adult like a tree grows into its roots, the fruits of summer begin to allow the soul to expand further in their own identity of "who they are". Teenagers throughout this summer period of their lives may seem to be more carefree and loving towards one another than previously experienced. The days are longer and the essence of fun makes life enjoyable for most.

Throughout the summer period the innocence of the spring season is over and the harsher conditions of life begin to present themselves. Teenagers may experience more heated moments, taking a little longer for them to cool down. The thirst for self-identity and recognition is more evident as they seek differences in living through experimentation of various methods.

As the soul begins to settle in life and form its own place of living and family unit, the leaves on the tree that have swayed so carefree in the wind now begin to fall. Autumn has arrived and the roots are now comforted with nourishment from the leaves that once believed the sky was the limit. There is a recognition that what was once considered possible to achieve now seems to be less probable as responsibilities have deepened the roots into the ground.

This penetration of growth into the earth can trigger the soul seeking a balance in the spiritual aspects of life. They seem to have greater physical responsibilities than ever before, resulting in higher levels of stress and anxiety. The top part of the tree wants to be nurtured again even though the leaves may now be gone.

There is a knowing within the soul that the branches still exist and they too have the capability of viewing life from a more stable platform. There is an understanding that the branches have always been there but seem to have been forgotten as part of the nurturing process. Now that the roots are stable, the feelings in the higher branches can be experienced once more.

As the branches begin to activate again like signals within the brain, there is a knowingness of connectivity that was never lost. Souls begin to reach out further to other souls. When a branch breaks and falls back into the earth, there is a seeking of answers into the physical death process. This seeking of the branch falling results in further soul progression and understanding of "who you are".

As winter arrives on the horizon, the fragility of life is evident. More and more branches fall off the tree and in time the connectivity of souls that once existed on earth is no longer visible to the human eye. There is an understanding that they never truly died but simply transformed into new life. These souls reside in a place that is far deeper in understanding of what life is all about, as experienced by all cycles within the universe.

Death

Death is a topic that is often avoided, particularly in Western societies. It is something that is mostly discussed only at the time of the process itself, causing panic and confusion when it does appear on the doorstep. The deep sadness that most people feel with this physical departure causes a misconception of what the actual process is all about. It leaves many in despair and suffering long-term cycles of grief.

If one knew what death was in the first place and had an understanding of its purpose, a lot of the stages of grief could be dealt with on a new level. Many people feel the emotions of anger and denial and would like to blame an outside party or higher force for the departure of a loved one. In some instances, the fault of another person may well be the cause of the death, but for all souls a life plan has already been laid out.

Death can be seen as a simple process of walking from one room to another. At the moment of physical death the soul transcends into another dimension that vibrates at a higher frequency than the earth plane. Life now resides in a non-material world that operates at a deeper level of mental and emotional activity that has not been experienced through life on earth.

Each individual will experience death differently depending on the circumstances of their departure and emotional and spiritual wellbeing at the time. A sudden death will require adjustment on the other side through healing provided by friends, relatives and helpers who specialise in this area of need. Long-term illness can provide the soul with preparation before making the final transition to their new life.

The grief stages of bargaining and depression for the soul making transition into the spirit world can be experienced on a more subtle level if a person understands their own contractual agreement in their life whilst on earth. Once a soul takes ownership for choosing their own experiences before incarnating into their physical life, acceptance of physical death as a part of this process can be more comforting for those souls.

A journey through a physical life on earth is not much different to a journey on the other side. A soul makes decisions about what they wish to achieve and experience in their existence, including the players they wish to involve and interact with. A decision to network with other souls and meet like-minded spirits has an unconscious knowingness that these relationships are dynamic and never static. Change is always inevitable.

At some stage the soul moves onto another plane of existence in the hope of progressing in the understanding of "who they are". Past relationships are never lost but are simply a reminder of the activation of "who you are". Only through the departure of souls from one life to the next can an individual recognise certain aspects of their personality that otherwise may have remained dormant throughout life.

Physical death is required for the soul to move from attempting to experience "who they are" to accepting "who they are" upon transition into the spirit world. A loss of the physical body removes the mask of unwanted feelings of identity that existed on the earth plane whilst interacting with other souls. In this moment the soul becomes powerful in the knowing that nothing can ever harm it and all life is interconnected through energy.

Each and every day souls change their outlook, appearance and love for one another depending on their current perceptions. These shifts in the recognising of "who you are" are all cycles of death within themselves and should not be seen as foreign to physical death. Death is simply the closing of one's perspective of life and the opening of new possibilities of experiencing it again with different souls who are progressing in a similar manner.

Direction

Throughout your life there will be times when you will feel that your thoughts and actions are not helping you progress towards the goals you wish to pursue. You may have expectations that a certain path needs to be followed in order to achieve a specific result. However most of the time what is not considered are the varying factors in life that you do not have control over.

It is easy to believe that everything you set out to achieve can manifest in the form that you desire. But what is important to realise is that the path towards this manifestation process will require many players apart from just you. These other people will also have their own expectations and plans which are dynamic and ever-changing.

The key to creating the life you truly deserve is to surrender to all possibilities and paths that open along your journey. As you set out to discover "who you are", you will also see that life is full of surprises and it is these wonders that will fulfil the joy and happiness within your soul. Attempting to plan and control the rays beaming towards the sunset will only limit your own light in the expansion of your true identity.

Trust and surrender are very important teachers in your life. Learning to let go and embrace the unknown allows your spirit to guide your experience in the physical world. You will understand that your soul is not confined to time and space and has the ability to inspire your earthly life in a way that is favourable to yourself and others.

There are many paths in the course of life that allow you to learn from different experiences. You can embrace certain aspects of yourself that otherwise may have remained undiscovered throughout this life. Other souls may be guided into your direction at a time you least expected in order to assist in the fulfilment of these dreams.

Once you realise you are much more than a physical body, the direction of your life will change in many ways. Instead of attempting to control the winding paths along your way, you will embrace the different viewpoints and see the beauty in all the ups and downs. You will know that today is more important than tomorrow or yesterday, and your current experience is exactly where it should be now.

There are many different directions, paths and major roads that can be taken in your life. Some are more difficult than others and require navigational assistance along the way. Others can take you in the opposite direction, leaving you feeling off-course. In those instances a reliance on your intuition and soul satellite is required for you to feel your way back.

Do not allow others to tell you that your life has no meaning or direction. Do not even say it to yourself. Ultimately, all roads can eventually lead to your destination with perhaps some of them requiring more effort and energy than others. When you are connected to "who you are" and have an acceptance of your unlimited abilities, you can achieve anything your soul wishes to pursue in this lifetime.

Discipline

The art of discipline is something that humans have struggled with for many years. The ability to focus the mind throughout the creation process requires the concentrating of energy in a particular vibration. Self-doubt and lack of self-worth do not assist you in remaining focused on the tasks at hand and only create setbacks in the discovery path of "who you are".

Those who are self-driven enough to achieve certain goals in life have an understanding that you are responsible for creating your own reality. They do not rely on the people around them to provide them with continuous energy and support in the hope that everything will magically come together without effort. Believing that life should be seamless and requiring no work at all would be ignorant to the sole purpose of its existence.

Your internal motivation should be aligned with the overall intention of what you have set out to achieve. If your intentions are purely of a material sense, with little consideration for the wellbeing of others, then souls will not be drawn to assist you on your path of self-indulgence and over-empowerment. It is important that you are disciplined enough throughout your life that constant self-reflection occurs on what is important to your spiritual journey as well as your material life.

Discipline needs to stem from your mind, body and spirit. If you feed one area without supplementing the other an imbalance can occur, resulting in further over-compensation and exhaustion in the long run. By allowing yourself to exercise and eat correctly on a daily basis, your vessel will be fuelled with enough energy and substance to keep you going.

Your mind should be open enough to allow new philosophies, possibilities and methods of thinking into your life. By grasping new concepts and ideas, you become a channel for inspiration in the quest for seeking further information and guidance from your own soul and the souls of others. You will have an understanding of the greater purpose in life, allowing you to navigate a healthier route on the path of self-discovery.

The mind should also be subjected to silence. This does not mean complete quietness in an auditory sense. Quietness within the mind exists when human ego thoughts are not attempting to analyse the past or future in a manner of attempting to seek control. It is when you are able to seize a moment and lose the concept of time and space amongst the wonders of creation.

Silencing of the mind can occur through various methods other than just meditation. Gardening, painting, singing, walking, swimming and reading can provide you with this state of bliss. It is where you are able to discipline yourself enough to make a decision to focus your attention elsewhere in the hope of experiencing the now. Over time you will find yourself switching off from the outside world and into the essence of your own spirit.

True discipline is where a person can connect with their own spirit at any one point in time. Distractions and noises from the physical world do not impede their ability to blend with their higher self or the souls of others both in the physical and spiritual realms. They understand the greater purpose of life and know that energy can produce wonderful results when used in a disciplinary manner. Once you believe something is achievable, you simply need to focus your mindset on creating it as part of your reality.

Doubt

Doubt is something that many know to exist but have difficulty recognising the part it plays in holding a soul back throughout its life journey. It's the voice in one's mind through words or feelings that give the impression that further action or lack of action is required moving forward. It will also venture over past events and provide feelings of regret or remorse for the life that has been led so far here on the earth plane.

Doubt is very different to having initial reservations about something based on gut feelings and trust. Going with the first thoughts that enter the mind with little judgement of the situation or the persons at hand will almost always come from the higher part of one's self. This part of yourself knows what is best for you in this life and will always take the path that is of the greatest benefit for your greater plan.

When a person is constantly subjected to a negative environment with non-positive mindsets surrounding them, it is easy for the lower ego of the human self to want to engage in paranoid thoughts of lower vibrations. These thoughts may be projected to you as ideas coming from someone else that you feel to be true of them. You may be convinced this is what they think of you when in fact it may well be your own perception of their reality based on ego thoughts created in your own mind.

So many misconceptions occur on the earth plane due to mistruths of perceptions of one's reality. If your mind is not connected to your true spirit, which is of love, truth and forgiveness, then it is difficult for you to believe that others are of joy, trust and kindness towards you. Before you allow your mind to create lower vibration thoughts of yourself or others, first ask yourself where all this energy is coming from.

It is easy to be caught up in the energy of your own human ego attempting to destroy any possibilities that are presented to you throughout your earthly lives. If you have other minds around you that are willing to participate in these doubtful thoughts, then penetration of your mind with further doubt can occur. You can then disconnect from your spirit and ultimately in the discovery of "who you are".

Often upon a life review at physical death, a soul will almost always feel levels of regret that they did not enjoy life enough and take so many of the opportunities that were presented to them. Self-doubt is very powerful. It is like a virus that changes its form constantly to avoid recognition and therefore a cure. It is highly contagious and often presents itself as something that it is truly not. It requires a host in the physical body to survive and that host is simply your own human ego.

Through positive stimulation of the mind, body and spirit, a cure for self-doubt can be discovered as the infection of negative thoughts will not even enter your energy field. It will have nothing to align itself with as your higher vibration of energy will provide greater discipline over your human ego thoughts. Doubt can be something that can be replaced more and more by positive gut feelings and trust in "who you are".

Dreams

Dreams give you feelings of hope that one day you will achieve something far greater than presently experienced in the physical world. They can provide you with a benchmark of what is possible in your life for something that currently seems out of reach on the horizon of your reality.

The sharing of dreams with others can be just as exciting as the possibility of the eventual experience. The journey in attempting to achieve certain goals over a given period of time can bring about a sense of urgency and excitement that perhaps may have felt missing throughout your life. There is a knowing that one day the activation of thought into a real physical experience is quite probable, even against the greatest odds that you may feel.

Dreams provide hope and inspiration to people in their everyday lives. Often other souls are involved in the activation process and encouragement of those initial thoughts when creating the mapping of the mindset of the soul. It is important that the person never loses hope in their original intentions. Love from those in both the physical and spiritual worlds play an important role in the nurturing of someone's dream.

There is not much difference between the wanting of something in the physical world through initial mental thought and the creation of another reality in the dream state whilst sleeping. Both experiences involve the mind extending itself beyond the capabilities of matter on the earth plane. The soul has the ability in any dream state to rise above the laws of physics and see the greater possibilities that are at hand.

When the soul shifts its perception beyond the material world limitations, then true joy, love and inspiration can be experienced. Whilst in these states of bliss, there is a forgetting of what is not possible and rather a reminder of what is possible. The spirit does not constantly stop and question its reality but rather embraces the moments of connectivity that may only be experienced momentarily whilst in the physical body.

Whether these moments of happiness are experienced whilst sleeping or daydreaming, it does not matter. The feelings of love and encouragement are felt by those in realms beyond the material world and a sureness in "who you are" is discovered at these wonderful times.

The questioning of the source of this inspiration as coming from your own spirit or others is irrelevant. In moments of connectivity between souls of various realms, the meeting of loved ones can leave an imprint within you that is everlasting. You may not be able to remember the faces of those you connected with but there is an instant recognition of love that is identified through vibrations.

The dream state can be very powerful in providing a wonderful forum for the gathering of many souls. Not only can inspiration and encouragement transpire into action but feelings of grief and loss can quickly subside. Your loved ones may come to you with a message or even a projection of themselves in a happy and peaceful state. This can provide great hope and comfort that no physical experience on earth could ever replace.

Eclipse

To embark on any journey in life you need to be willing to take the high and the low roads in order to understand the purpose of the ride. Sometimes it is easy to hold on to moments throughout the journey that were perhaps less bumpy or to emphasise those sections that made you feel as though you were outside your comfort zone.

It is more likely that these extreme moments will be captured in memory rather than the stiller parts of the journey. It is human nature to believe that if something is too good then it is bound to turn negative at some point in time. This type of attitude can leave behind a lack of gratitude, causing less fortunate events to be attracted to you. It is important to maintain a balanced perspective on both positive and negative experiences and see the greater eclipse in it all.

When there is an eclipse in something there is always a section where the light and dark must overlap. This blending of energy together brings about a unity and oneness in the understanding that all situations, whether they are considered to be of light or dark nature, eventually must come together. This attraction between opposing viewpoints is where the greatest learning from any circumstance or event can be achieved.

It is often through adversity that you are able to eventually see the light in your life. Sometimes you may take things for granted along the ride until you discover that the tracks are not always secure or withstanding of sudden movements or changes. These discoveries often leave you in a reflection mode long enough for you to review your journey and the greater plan of life.

Throughout the ride you may discover that those you have carried on the journey may not be supportive in the challenging parts of your life. You perhaps did not enjoy the time you previously spent together on the smoother sections but managed to ignore the truth since there was no reason to change the course. It is only through forced change that you can be required to reassess your passengers and those who may have taken over the wheel on certain times of the ride.

On the hillier, more unstable parts of the journey, you may find that your viewpoint of upcoming twists and turns is evident on the horizon. Previously, it may have been blocked by other passengers but clarity of truth has come forth. The light that shines on the valleys and mountains ahead brings you peace in the knowing that you can take control of your own life through free will and choice.

Throughout the journey, there will be sections of tunnels that will require you to surrender and believe in yourself. In order to get to the wonderful scenic route, complete darkness may be required for your inner guidance to shine through. The blending parts of the eclipse are not too far away as your carriageway in life breathes new air as it exits the tunnel.

As you move out of the darkness and into the light, you will have a greater understanding of yourself and your journey ahead. You will know that you are the greatest guide in your life and there will always be breathtaking opportunities. Embracing this understanding of the eclipse of life is a sure ticket to knowing "who you are" and what you have come to the earth plane for.

Emotion

Sometimes in life your emotions can be so strong that you may feel out of balance. It is important that you attempt to be aware of the source of those emotions so you learn to accommodate for changes in the environment and people around you. You do not need to try to control these emotions as there is a reason why you are feeling them in the first place.

Often people feel more hormonal and emotional at certain cyclical times of the year. Women tend to be more aware of their flows in energy and on some occasions consciously attempt to be mindful of how they respond and react throughout those times. Through understanding that you are a combination of mind, body and spirit you will find that your coping mechanisms will be that of a more positive responsive manner than that of a negative one.

Exercising your body stimulates the oxygen levels in the blood, allowing you to feel more rejuvenated and refreshed. If your emotions are running high, it provides you with an opportunity to release the energy from the body whilst at the same time giving your mind a potential meditative state to process your thoughts. In those moments you can become instantly aware of the source of your feelings.

Once you acknowledge that you are feeling emotional, this will provide your mindset with a type of permission to surrender and release. Sometimes the soul can be connecting unconsciously to past thoughts or actions or picking up on emotions and feelings outside of itself. Empathising with others can trigger certain feelings that you may misinterpret as your own.

On some occasions, it can be energy that is residual and collective in the conscious thought of animals and other life, including humans. The moon can also have an influence on the emotions of living things on earth. Emotions are a way for energy to express itself through feeling rather than speaking.

In a lot of the societies that exist on the earth today, emotions are viewed as a weaker part of the human personality. Some people believe an emotional character to be irrational and not capable of making proper decisions. The less emotional a person is, the more they may be considered to be of leadership status, which carries an essence of the human ego itself.

Like all energy flows that operate on earth, a balance is required to live a healthy and sustainable life. A physical existence requires the ability to think in a survival mode and love and care for yourselves and your fellow human beings. Being empathetic towards others is important in the understanding of the connectivity and oneness of all life.

Ensuring that your mind, body and spirit are aligned as much as possible allows you to process and identify the source of your current thoughts, actions and feelings. This insight encourages you to embrace "who you are" in the hope that it inspires others to do the same. Do not be embarrassed of your feelings and emotions as they are as valid in expressing "who you are" as thoughts and words that project from your mind and body.

Energy

To understand the forces of nature and the cycles of life you first must know and accept that all that exists is sourced from the flow of energy. Energy is the essence of all that ever was and will be. Nothing can be created without the flow of this into the source of initial thoughts and actions on varying vibrations.

Birds, animals, plants and ecosystems work together intensively in the hope that their energy can be sustained through interdependency. Reliance stems from an underlying instinct that all life is interconnected.

Human beings perceive energy very differently to other beings on earth. Some believe that in order to benefit themselves, someone or something else needs to be sacrificed. There seems to be a loss in the understanding that energy can never be destroyed but only transformed. Energy will always change its structure but will never completely disappear in nature.

All energy, once amalgamated and combined with other energy, becomes part of something greater. This larger combination of forces can bring about wonderful experiences and creations. By uniting this intelligence from different fields of study, new possibilities and avenues can be discovered to bring about positive future changes for the earth and its inhabitants.

Once the spirit becomes inspired enough to encourage new ideas and concepts, the struggles then begin in the delivery of the thoughts into the world of matter. The human ego can discourage new thought patterns and methods in the hope that it will go away and remain dormant in the minds where creation first began. The desire for power in the unfolding process may bring about negative feelings such as jealousy and envy towards others.

Having negative thoughts towards yourself or others lowers the vibration of your energy field. Over time you may feel less connected with "who you are" and more disconnected with others. This results in lower levels of energy both emotionally and mentally which in time begins to affect the physical body. You may then feel the side effects of fatigue, tiredness and ill health.

It is important that you view yourself as beings of light and energy. Do not just see "who you are" as a physical person living a life in a world of matter. Every part of you is energy and always will be energy regardless of which side of life you reside on. Through physical death your soul's consciousness will continue on through your energy field that is currently connected to your physical body.

So much energy is required on a daily basis to maintain your mind, body and spirit. When you are feeling depressed, sad or angry, ask yourself where the deprivation of energy may be coming from. Once you understand that your energy levels need to be attended to, then you will be able to maintain a happy and healthy life. Through exercise, friendly eating, quiet time and self-love, you will find that your energy levels can be maintained and restored, allowing you to live a fulfilled life.

Experience

Most human beings want to experience many things in life. Having an experience on an emotional, spiritual or physical level almost always leaves the soul wondering what the experience would have been like if one small factor was different. Something that may have been considered to be a minor input in the experience can have a major impact on the outcome.

Experience can be viewed from two main levels. It can be viewed through the growing of a person from beginner to advanced on specific knowledge or expertise in a particular area of discipline. The second level of observation is through the soul's path of progression in learning and revealing certain aspects of oneself. Both levels can be intertwined into the experience itself where conscious observation does not cause any level of distinction.

By interacting with other souls in your life, you can obtain indirect knowledge and learning without being involved in the experience itself. Being of open heart and open mind removes barriers of lack of self-love and self-worth. This allows you to be receptive to new learning that otherwise could have been closed down through underlying thoughts of arrogance and ignorance.

Many people walk through life without the understanding that life itself is an experience. Each and every day, new variables enter the equation of the life contract, creating both wonderful and challenging moments. Your experience is also someone else's experience, and by projecting your loving and creative thoughts onto others, you are affecting other souls' lives in their progression as well.

If you limit "who you are" in life, then you are limiting your life experiences greatly. The more you reveal "who you are" through truth, the more truthful your experiences will be. Alignment of thought and action in the physical world occurs when truth itself exists on all three levels. If the mind, body and spirit of the person are in sync with one another, then your experiences can be ones of heightened levels of joy and happiness.

Two separate people can enter a room and be exposed to identical circumstances but walk away with different experiences. The perception of what has occurred in the room is of critical nature when assessing the outcome of the experience. If one perceives the people in the room to have negative and judgemental behaviour, then that is what they will ultimately experience themselves.

If a person projects love and light into a situation regardless of the thoughts and actions projected around them then their life experiences will always be of a positive nature. These people have an understanding that thoughts create their reality and if they maintain a positive mindset then their reality can certainly be one of happiness despite what is going on around them.

Expertise in a certain area of discipline does not guarantee a positive experience. Someone of open heart and open mind with little knowledge can bring forward inspirational ideas that can change past patterns of behaviour. By having limited previous experience, the mind is not rejecting different and new possibilities of learning. These new methods of learning can be fun, rewarding and exciting for others to experience on their soul-seeking path as well.

Experience is not something that should be measured by time and space. It is an ongoing process that the soul encounters throughout its life with ever-changing reflections of "who you are". Your experience can empower others to change their current ways of thinking and from this the earth can be a more peaceful place for all souls wishing to have a memorable physical life experience.

Faith

The common factor amongst all religions and belief systems is faith. There is a knowing that something or someone outside of yourselves is guiding and assisting you throughout your earthly lives. This inner trust can be in energetic forms unrecognisable to some people depending on their interpretation of "God".

The key to all faith is trust. There is a trust that a greater purpose exists for all. This purpose if true in light should not judge, segregate or despise other belief systems. It should reveal itself as being open and honest at all times with a feeling of love, joy and connectivity to all humanity and its fellow inhabitants on earth. Trust should always share with it the essence of truth.

When you live a life of truth, there is no need to be consciously aware of trust. Only when you have thoughts of mistruths and injustices will you then experience issues of trust both within yourself and with those surrounding you. If someone is not expressing truth to you then it is your choice whether to engage further in the mistrusting thoughts and actions.

Often people say that they do not trust themselves around certain people, actions or events. They do not have the faith to stand strong in their own self to see the truth. This confrontation with oneself can be overwhelming, especially when a person has lost contact with "who they are". A disconnection can result in further segregation which can cause a loss of faith in not just themselves but humanity as a whole.

It is normally through hardship and adversity that true faith is tested. Many can take the option to blame this outside force for all the wrongdoings that have occurred in the past. Others may see it as an opportunity to allow certain events and actions beyond themselves to shape "who they are". Either way, faith itself can bring both light and darkness into thought processes, depending on the balance of the human ego.

Under extreme circumstances, the human mind has the capability to believe that it is the greatest being alive on the earth plane, connecting to a superior force unreachable to many. These thought patterns are indicators of an ego that is self-indulgent and self-empowering to the extent where all other belief systems are incorrect.

You should always be mindful of your own thoughts and actions as well as those of the people around you. Do not be influenced by outside forces that promote hate and lack of unity within your communities. Do not view these minds to be powerful and correct in their interpretation of "God". Use your common sense when interpreting the greater faith of the human race.

All faith from light can heal and bring joy to many if it vibrates on the feelings of love, joy and happiness. Regardless of its representation, faith will always promote the values of trust, truth and connectivity. These values are the essence to the ingredients of world peace. It is only when humanity can identify these as being of importance, that the earth plane can exist in a more giving and balanced nature.

Family

All human beings when entering the physical world need to be taken care of by at least one person in order to survive. In most cases this role is undertaken by parents but for some souls their journey begins with people who may not even be blood related. Either way, it is important that souls feel they are part of someone or something far greater than themselves. It is this feeling of being a part of the whole in the human race that gives meaning to the term "family".

Feeling a part of the whole is important for a soul in recognising "who they are". Only through the interaction and learning with others can you fully understand all aspects of your own personalities. The dynamics of the family unit encourage growth in different phases of your life from childhood to adolescence and finally through to adulthood. Often family members will come together or move apart throughout the varying stages of life but ultimately there will always be a connection to the family on a deeper soul level.

The family unit that was chosen for you to be born into serves a higher purpose in your life. Characters of differing ages, sexes and personalities will bring out what you may consider to be the best and worst within your own personality. These degrees of self-judgement and judgement of others in the family unit will change over time depending on the learning phase within each of the family members.

Some of the learning phases will overlap and you may find yourself saying, "I feel as though I am living the life of so and so." This may well be the case with your life replicating a part of the family unit behaviour based on genetics, environment or an overriding feeling of fear. When one fears becoming a certain person, these thoughts can be placed into the mind over and over to the extent that a level of programming occurs.

The projection of your thoughts into the universe is something that you need to be mindful of. Universal laws of cause and effect do not identify what is right or wrong for you but simply execute what you wish to create as part of your own reality. If through fear you do not wish to create a certain life based on past family values or attitudes, be aware not to place too much energy into these thoughts.

Instead of constantly judging yourself and those around you within the family structure, embrace every part of yourself and attempt to accept "who you are". Do not be embarrassed by the genetics that have been given to you but rather accept them as chosen gifts that were necessary for your life path of learning. What you may consider to be dysfunctional in your family unit may well be quite functional in obtaining the challenges required for your own soul growth and the growth of others.

Always attempt to understand new members who enter your family unit. Remember that their genetics, environment and attitudes towards life may be different but ultimately it is the love and support that you can give to one another that is of importance. Each and every day, attempt to make other souls feel as though they are a part of your family by judging less and embracing as many aspects of "who you are" through the soul exchange process.

Fear

Fear is so powerful on earth that it controls a lot of the decisions and actions undertaken in many human lives. It is an emotion that spreads like a highly contagious disease that can take hold of a person's mind and leave them paralysed in their thought processing patterns. It can also leave souls feeling worthless.

Increasing technology in many parts of the world is fuelling the growth of fear. Through media, the quickening speed of sharing information can result in a lack of truth. The deep network of underlying motives and intentions can poison the flow of truth which can lead many to believe that the perception on the surface is the actual reality of the world.

Fear within a soul can remain dormant for many years without resurfacing. The person may have no idea why they feel a certain way towards specific actions, people or circumstances. Their response may well be one of a reaction instead of an interaction, leading to further problems and complications in the establishment of new relationships in their lives.

Normally the birthing of fear results from the implant of a thought into a person's mind with an underlying negative tone of vibration. The soul somehow does not have the ability to convince the human ego that it is much stronger than these initial thoughts. Rather, it decides to feed these primary thoughts with secondary thoughts resulting in the incubation of more fear over time.

If a person really knows "who they are", they would battle less with the struggles between the human ego and the spirit. They would understand that nothing can ever harm them, including physical death, and all roads in life lead to greater learning and understanding of the self. They would know that lack of self-love results in high levels of fear and this can be combated by giving oneself more love.

Do not entertain fearful thoughts and actions if you wish to live a life of a more positive and loving nature. Choose not to surround yourself with negative media or individuals and organisations that promote lack of self-worth or harm to others. It is normally when the human mind is in fear mode that it acts out as a form of protection against itself and others.

Ask yourself who or what has inspired you in life to become a better person in the discovery path of "who you are"? Take this reflection as your oxygen tanks of survival and allow yourself to resurface constantly. Once your tanks become large enough, feed others with this clean air and give permission to your own soul to shine.

Feelings

When someone asks you about your feelings, normally there is a pause. The mind will automatically scan your thoughts to see what is acceptable to share and what will be judged by others. When asked how you actually feel, it can bring about feelings of discomfort and further exposure.

When we speak of feeling, what does it actually mean? It seems to be a very relaxing word with a flow about it, like the energy of an emotion. It is not something that can be measured, controlled or even completely revealed but it seems to operate at a much deeper level in decision making processes throughout your life.

You may hear your mind say: "I feel like a hamburger", "I feel it is too cold to go outside" or "I feel that so and so is just not himself at the moment". In each of these instances, you have more than likely not even seen a hamburger, ventured outside into the weather or made contact with the person at hand. So how do you know this information through your feelings? Something is operating at another level that you are not even aware of when you hear these words in your mind.

Feelings do not necessarily need to carry with them a sense of emotion. They are a knowing about a person, situation, object or any form of energetic vibration that exists throughout various planes of existences. They are a sense of connection to this energetic bond that brings about a thought in the mind that influences the overall decision-making process.

Once the attention has been brought to the fore about a particular feeling, then variances in emotions can be witnessed thereafter depending on the connectivity of those around the particular person. If, for instance, someone is feeling deep levels of grief, different levels of emotions will come to the surface, depending on who the person is asking the question: "How do you feel?" At this point, the mind will then take over and decide the level of truth to be revealed about the feeling.

The more relaxed a person is, alone or around other people, the more likely it is that the truth will be exposed on how they feel. If the person does not feel judged by another or is not experiencing self-judgement, then more than likely they will be able to express to their greatest ability how their mind is interpreting what is going on inside their heart.

This is why so many people throughout their earthly lives seek the services of counsellors and social workers. It is healthy to open your hearts and minds to others without feeling judged. The creation of the feeling in the beginning was through an initial source of energy, so the healing may involve others as well.

Remember to allow your heart to process your feelings truthfully and continue to express yourself in your everyday life. Simply allow you to just be and let your own experience in life be a heartfelt one for both yourself and those connected to you through the wonderful web of life.

Food

The source of all life is energy. In the physical world, food is an important factor in the sustainability of life for the plant, animal and human species. It is something that should be considered as one of the highest priorities in preservation. Preserving of one's energy for the greater consciousness of the planet should be experienced by souls when incarnating on the earth plane.

The world has enough energy in food form to feed the entire planet with ease. So much waste occurs on a daily basis especially in the Western parts of the planet. Continued free will and choice in the consumption of food has increased the variety of the sources available causing many to feel there is an over-abundance of food available. This misconception is not of truth but many feel that starvation is a cause of death only in the past.

If governments and organisations across the world worked more closely together in attempting to achieve equality, starvation could easily be made into something of a distant memory. Many souls spend their days working in fields to find themselves with the inability to feed their own families. Exportation of large amounts of food from less privileged countries to more enriched ones leaves these people with feelings of despair and lack of hope.

By encouraging those in political power to provide these areas of the world with seeds for personal growth of food, families can work together more closely and a variety and abundance of food can be experienced by all with minimal waste. It is difficult to remove free trade globally on food products so it is necessary to assist those in local communities to trade amongst themselves with some level of power and agreement.

Empowering people through education, tools and the seeds of plant life also educates yourself through the exchanges of energy in giving and receiving. By ensuring that other human beings are not exploited, you will soon discover the exploring of your own self and 'who you are'. This can be a wonderful journey for many on the path of self discovery.

Food can be a very important source of medicine for the physical body. Simply by consuming a variety of vitamins and minerals, the vessel you reside in has the ability to self-heal where necessary. Good sources of food also provide the brain with nutrition, leaving the mind at greater levels of peace. Without realising it, the mind, body and spirit can align once more and provide clarity to your existence.

When consuming food, it is important that you give gratitude to the physical matter itself as well as the energy of its initial life. Being grateful for all things in life is important especially when attempting to recognise the cycles of energy that exist in everything you do and experience. Food is a simple example in training your mind to give thanks and in time you can extend this to family, friends and the greater planet and its inhabitants.

Forgiveness

In order to forgive a certain person, action or circumstance you must first recognise that the energy you are carrying needs to be released. Only then are you able to identify the underlying feelings and emotions that are holding you back in life. Forgiveness does not mean that you are agreeing with the nature of the energy, you are simply choosing to no longer carry it with your life experience.

The human mind has a way of telling itself that forgiveness means you have given up. It will provide you with the impression that you are the weaker one and have chosen to surrender to the energy. But the key word here is surrender. Surrender and trust are of much higher vibrations in truth than anger, denial and frustration. These lower vibrations can eventually leave you unwell on mental, physical and emotional levels.

Over many years, continuous feelings of hatred, resentment and disconnection can leave the person experiencing very little in life. They can eventually shut themselves off from the rest of humanity, hoping that people will just go away and life will become bearable. The concept of surrender is not on the agenda. This creates limited possibilities and restricted hope for new beginnings.

If you are feeling hurtful and untrusting of the human experience, ask yourself whether you believe that all life operates on such a level. Have a few experiences clouded your judgement on the greater gifts that simply existing can offer you? Has a certain person inflicted pain not only on your life but perhaps on others through their indirect effects of negative energy?

It is up to you if you choose to allow energy that was originally contaminated to continue to poison your lives. By not feeding the pollution with further time and effort, you can make certain choices and actions that can release your energy into clarification and purification. It does not mean that the pollution no longer exists, you have just chosen to no longer live and breathe in a toxic environment.

Once you understand that forgiveness breaks away the energetic ties you have with whatever it is, then you will know that your lives can become much lighter and brighter in the future. If past situations were traumatic for you, don't allow this to continue on and take over the rest of your life. By breaking and releasing the energy, it is up to the other parties to deal with the cause and effect of their own actions.

Sometimes forgiving yourself is just as important as forgiving others. The human mind can hold on to energy and manipulate thoughts to the extent that it creates a reality based on self-judgement. Punishing "who you are" can give you a type of permission to self-destruct and possibly self-harm which serves no purpose at all.

Unfortunately, life will encounter many players and circumstances that can be very unfavourable. It is not the other people or situations that are of importance, it is you. It is how you decide to lead your life moving forward in the direction that you wish to live. If your current thoughts and actions do not permit you to experience these wonders, then let them go as each and every one of you deserves to live a happy and fulfilling life.

Freedom

When freedom is spoken of, what does it actually mean? What is it that humans wish to be free from? Is it free from your own thoughts and actions that you place on yourself or the thoughts or actions of those around you? Freedom does not only refer to the release of physical captivation but also the expansion of the mind and spirit that feeds the creativity of life.

When you are free of impediments placed on the mind, body and spirit, the soul has the ability to shine like never before and become a beacon of light for itself as well as others observing its actions. It is this expansion in a carefree manner that brings forth inspiration on many levels within the human psyche.

Freedom allows you to become someone who has no limits in either time or space and your childlike characteristics will surface to the extent that others may observe you to be a little eccentric. You will seek answers to questions you may never have asked and in time a little part of you will begin to search new philosophies and possibilities like never before.

You may even become a pioneer in your field of work or an observer of brilliance unfolding before your own eyes. You may be called upon to be a messenger of this new inspiration and from this your spirit will shine. Your knowingness throughout the search for truth will reveal in time "who you are".

Through freedom, fellow human beings are no longer your competitors. A fight for food, clothing and shelter is not required in the physical world for freedom places equality across all souls. Freedom of speech will allow every soul to speak their truth and from this the human consciousness will expand.

Freedom of the human spirit is of utmost importance in the rise of the planet's consciousness. Segregation of souls based on judgements of belief systems will dissolve into a mass connectivity of knowingness that all is one.

Once there is an understanding of this connectivity at the soul level, inner peace will be restored through many lives. In time this will filter through governments and organisations to combat poverty and increase human rights. Through spiritual freedom, changes will then flow on to the human race in the physical world with differences between varying economies becoming marginally smaller on earth.

Free Will

It is often asked how much of your lives are predetermined and how much of it is created along the physical life journey. The answer to this question is very much dependent upon the connectivity between your own mind, body and spirit as well as your greater connectivity to others.

If someone lives a life of truth, love and joy they will discover that their life path will be aligned with "who they are". They will have no expectations of what should have been and what will be, but rather enjoy the now that is given to them on a day-to-day basis. This gratitude for the present allows them to surrender to their greater spirit, or higher self as you may know it.

If one understands they are a powerful being that is connected to humanity on a broader level, their attitude towards themselves and others will carry a sense of ownership and responsibility for current thoughts and actions. This requires an acceptance that you are what you think and your own free will and choices can indeed affect the outcome of a particular event or circumstance.

All human beings incarnate onto the earth plane in an attempt to evolve and learn through their interaction and teachings with others. This progression path requires silencing of the mind to listen to the signals along the pathways of the greater life plan. Repetitive situations will arise in one's life if the soul has not grasped the basic learning of the previous exchange processes.

You can always choose to ignore through your own free will upcoming thoughts and actions that have the potential to progress you further in the understanding of "who you are". This level of arrogance and ignorance that is projected by the human ego can in time create delusion to the extent where all problems and roadblocks in your life are the result of the belief of forces outside of your own self.

It is when there is a lack of alignment between the internal and external thought forces that confusion between free will and choice will result. If the person believes that an external force known as the universe or God will punish them for certain actions then the mind will internalise this manifestation and produce the resulting outcome with ease.

If however the soul understands that its internal thoughts affect the greater thinking of the mass consciousness then it has the ability to understand that the lower physical human ego experience needs to connect to the greater spirit. It is when this connection occurs that the person understands their blueprint in life and executes it according to the plan of its higher self.

The higher self of you knows and understands that everything in life has a purpose. Your spirit has the ability to guide you through many different paths to ultimately arrive at the pivotal intersections in your life. Different avenues of free will and choices can be used to encourage you to the destination but the main intersections will be reached at some point in time.

These varying potential paths leading to the greater moments in your life are perhaps what you would term as your free will and choice. It is your life and it is up to you how you progress throughout your journey. Some of you will take the scenic route but ultimately still arrive at your destination. Others may enjoy the bumpy roads along the way in the discovery of "who they are".

There is no right or wrong, only a knowingness that your own spirit will always be there to guide you through your choices. It is your free will and it is important that you understand this. Other souls cannot take responsibility for your own thoughts and actions but can only simply encourage you to make choices that are favourable in identifying "who you are".

Frustration

Life through its peaks and troughs can leave behind a trail of frustrating periods. There are times when you may feel as though you are completely on your own with no-one hearing or responding to your requests. You may find yourselves judging situations much sooner into the decision-making process in the hope that quick results will be better than none at all.

Frustration can stem from your beliefs that what you have right in front of you is not right in your life. You feel as though something brighter is on the horizon but blocks on the mental, emotional and physical levels are preventing you from moving forward. You wish to exit out of the current situation as soon as you can so that new ways and methods can expose themselves clearly to you in good time.

But what if your current circumstances are right for you? Is it possible that the frustration may be stemming from the non-alignment between your spirit and your ego at the human level? Could there be a constant battle between your needs of the soul and the wants of the physical world experiences? If they are not in agreement with one another, this can cause a build-up of energy resulting in feelings of frustration.

The only way to discover what path is the best for you is to sit with yourself throughout these restless periods and listen to your own spirit. You will know through your intuition what the next course of action will be and if nothing comes to you immediately then trust that your guidance will be received in the right moment at the right time.

Never feel as though your feelings are irrelevant. Your emotions do matter in your life but it is important that you attempt to balance these with your mental, physical and emotional states. When you take care of your mind, body and spirit then events in your life will come together more naturally rather than you attempting to force them in one area.

Frustration can also stem from the fear of being too frightened to move forward when the situation feels favourable to you. You may find yourself reflecting on past experiences and circumstances with a sense that history will repeat itself so therefore there is no purpose in pursuing a new path. Removing these attitudes in thinking is critical in allowing your soul to guide your life moving forward.

In order to break down barriers you need to identify that they exist in the first place. Common signals of their existence are constant making of excuses before an event or circumstance even arises. If you find yourself thinking in this manner, attempt to send positive and re-assuring thoughts into your mind that you are worthy and deserving of happiness in your life.

Frustration is simply the creating of these hurdles and feeling too exhausted to overcome them. If you do not wish to face the obstacles that your human ego may have formed in your mind, then simply change lanes and continue along another path. In time you will realise that there are different options that can be taken to lead you to the same place. You just need to know in these moments when choices and decisions need to be made through your own intuition and feelings.

Gifts

The opening of a gift or present in one's life can bring about joy to both the giver and receiver. The wishing to fulfil one another's wants and needs can be a satisfying moment when observing the happiness of those involved in the exchange process. But what is the true gift that is actually exchanged? Is the gift in physical form of importance or is it the object of affection and underlying intention of the gift that is of greater significance?

In the material world, over time there has been a decline in the acknowledgement of the original thought that stems from the intention of providing the gift in the first place. Through commercialisation of specific dates on the calendar, there has been an enormous amount of pressure placed on society to conform as to when a gift exchange is necessary.

The making of gifts through love with one's hands can be a beautiful gesture in recognising another soul or revealing a part of your own self. Often when one passes into the spirit world, it is these small gifts and gestures that are remembered and not the purchasing of a specific product from a third party person or organisation. The exchange of gifts should be personable and heartfelt in a way that a touching of one another's soul is experienced.

The giving of gifts to strangers who may be in need is a wonderful experience that all souls should have the chance to be involved in. The donating of items to children in less fortunate parts of the world can bring about great levels of love and laughter which can fulfil a part of "who you are". You may remember the simplicity of your own childhood from basic items and the knowing that nothing else was required to fulfil your day with happiness.

A gift is not always that of material wealth. The most common gifts that are felt with high levels of gratitude are friendships without judgement. Knowing that you are not on your own in a particular circumstance or situation is a comfort that every human being is entitled to throughout their existence on earth. Giving yourself to someone in an emotional and non-physical manner can be a joy. You never forget souls who were there in your less fortunate cycles of life.

The balance between giving and receiving of gifts in both a material and non-material manner is of importance. The universal laws of cause and affect require a pendulum of energy exchange where all parties should mutually benefit from the greater purpose of the initial soul interaction. Attempting to dominate one area of this exchange over another will only cause emotional turmoil in relationships, resulting in the formation of disappointments and expectations.

Attempt to consciously avoid these expectations and disappointments in your life by stepping outside the parameters that have been set out by the current society you live in. Do not walk away from someone in need hoping they will be taken care of by someone else. Open your hearts and minds to one another constantly and enjoy the gifts that each and every one of you experience in your daily lives.

Giving

The act of giving is something that provides humanity with a warmth and understanding that we are much more than our individual selves. It allows the soul to connect with others in a way that may not have occurred through normal everyday activities.

To give to another soul allows you to express "who you are" in your own manner.

Often when one gives to another there can be expectations of a return in the exchange. Normally this can result in disappointment as the receiver may not be able to identify the emotional or material ties that the giver has created in their own mind. It is important that you assess your intentions when giving to others so that an underlying motive for self-gain is not the sole purpose.

True giving is the giving of your heart and mind to yourself and others. It provides nutrition in the expansion of the knowingness of "who you are" on many different levels. Through relationships, there is an opportunity to activate certain aspects of you based on the common and different interests or understandings of all parties involved. It allows you to explore various parts of yourself that perhaps may have remained dormant in this life.

It is important that you give to yourself on a daily basis. This giving should be a balance between the mind, body and spirit. The giving to yourself in a material sense will not provide you with happiness unless it is supplemented with soul food and the feeding of the hunger of the mind. No person can survive on physical world needs and wants without healthy thoughts and an ignited spirit.

There are some who have strong belief systems that they need to give to others constantly before they give to themselves. A balance is required to ensure that your own mind, body and spirit are not exhausted to the extent where you are not able to assist anyone any more, including yourself. Self-love is just as important as the giving of love to others.

If more people experienced the power of giving to others throughout their lives then the levels of depression and unhappiness on earth would be much less. By giving in an equal and balanced nature, the human race would embrace one another in a way that allows connectivity to be more achievable. The feelings of self-worth instead of self-gain could be understood, which would then allow every person the opportunity to embrace each other without judgement.

Often when one gives to another, a form of judgement is placed when the exchange process occurs. Based on your own past experiences or values, you may decide that a certain person is of greater need or worth over another soul. These judgements can be based on factors such as status, religion, race, age or sexuality. You may find your own self-worth is influencing the worthiness of others.

Over time you will more than likely realise through self-reflection that past judgements may have been more closed-minded. Throughout your daily decisions, try to attempt to use less judgement in the act of giving and more of a heartfelt response. Through this you will see that giving should be a gift from one soul to another.

Goodbye

There will be many times in your life where souls leave your path and you will never physically have the opportunity to say goodbye to them. Most of the time you will not be able to remember the last time you saw old friends, colleagues or acquaintances before they drifted out of your life. So what is the difference between the drifting of these souls out of your life to the exit of loved ones you hoped to say goodbye to before physical death?

There is a greater plan operating on guidance given by the universe as to what players should be entering and exiting your physical lives. Some souls are meant to be a part of your life for a short but perhaps more intensive period than others. This intensity can bring about new dynamics in your existing relationships which can further enhance the self-discovery of "who you are".

There are also times when a person may enter your life and you feel as though a level of intrusion has occurred. They may stir up feelings and emotions within you that cause heightened levels of fear and frustration. Others may observe you as being of difficult nature throughout this shorter period when in fact the time the soul has spent with you may well and truly be beyond your current physical lifetime.

Often when soul recognition occurs at first greeting, there is great opportunity for new learning to occur. This person may have been connected with you in a previous life or you spent time with them on the other side before incarnation into your current existence. Either way, you need to trust that a contractual agreement between you may be in operation and the lower human ego will need to surrender to this realisation at some point in time.

When connecting with new souls who enter your life, you will feel certain aspects of yourself that either resonate or repel upon meeting them. This is like attempting to mix freshwater and saltwater, they share a common substance but vary in salinity levels. Your awareness of life-survival skills will be dependent upon how far you are willing to swim in the unknown territory.

Venturing into the unseen is often associated with the physical death of your loved ones. In the moment of departure, there is a knowing that they are no longer physically there but there is a feeling that they have moved onto somewhere else. This other place will differ in your mind depending on the personality of those who have departed and your own self-belief systems.

If you accept in your mind that your loved ones have simply moved onto another journey then grief would be a little easier. Just as you know that friends and associates have drifted out of your life previously, there is a deeper understanding that this is natural and essential for the progression of souls in life. At some stage you will cross paths again, when the timing is correct for you both.

If you are physically bound by family ties and relationships, it would be unfair to assume that all souls are following the same path and learning as yourself. It is no different to children needing to grow up and move onto different schools and higher education. Loved ones have progressed as far as they can in this current lifetime and an exit has been chosen for their own higher purpose as well as yours. Trust in this purpose and soon you will realise that greetings and goodbyes are simply forks in the road on your own soul progression and that of others.

Gratitude

Gratitude is a word that is not often used in society today. You will sometimes hear people say thank you with an automatic response and little emotion in the words. True gratitude is heartfelt, where the recipient of the words will feel the exchange of appreciation between those involved. It is this exchange, connectivity and equality between souls that is the greatest gift of gratitude.

It is easy in the physical world to wake up in the morning and immediately think of all the tasks for the day. On very few occasions will people awake and say, "I give thanks for being alive and well today." It is assumed that life has just continued on from yesterday without the recognition that every day in the physical world is a blessing in itself. Once you recognise this blessing, your fulfilment will begin at the start of the day and you will not need to wait until the end of the day to experience something to make you happy.

Gratitude involves embracing every part of your life including yourself and those around you. It requires you to constantly look around and see that every person has been sent to you in this life as a gift. There are constant opportunities for you to grow and love yourself and each other. It is this love that allows you to expand and recognise "who you are".

Gratitude in the physical world involves appreciation on all the three levels: mentally, physically and spiritually. You need to give your mind a rest every now and then and appreciate the effort that it constantly makes to maintain your physical body functions as well as conscious thinking throughout the day. Your mind is a powerful tool but it also needs to be nurtured and cared for to ensure that a balance is achieved.

Your physical body is constantly subjected to everyday stresses and strains and should be considered when decisions are made to undertake any actions. Apart from external physical exposure, the human body is highly sensitive to certain chemicals and foods internally and should be taken care of at all times. An imbalance in one part of the body can cause problems holistically, requiring further treatments in the future.

Your physical environment, including your home, garden, animals and the planet itself need to be considered in your daily life. Ensuring that your air and water are kept clean with availability provided to all inhabitants is a part of recognising gratitude. Respecting that your life here is a temporary experience and others will need to inhabit your physical space in the future is of importance to everyone on the earth plane.

The diversity of culture, race and religion should be embraced as a gift of the human race instead of being seen as an opportunity for judgement of others. The uniqueness of every soul allows you the opportunity to activate certain aspects of "who you are". Crossing these aspects over can form beautiful blends of colours that otherwise may have never been discovered.

Gratitude allows you to blend together as one and to recognise that the human race is equal. Attempt to exchange more of this energy in your life and you will see that your heart will be filled with greater love and compassion. Your daily life will no longer just be bearable, but rather a wonderful joy of existence that will inspire many along their own journey in life.

Greetings

When you meet souls on your various pathways throughout life, never forget that all exchanges no matter how light or dark they may seem will progress you further in discovering "who you are". Each and every one of you has the power to give another soul the love and joy that individuals deserve throughout their physical lives.

Upon the first meeting with another human being, there can be the recognition of the spirit that resides within the physical body. This can be a familiarity of each other especially when connections are made upon eye contact. This beauty of identifying "who you are" can be moments you will treasure for the rest of your life.

Another soul has the ability to reflect to you the wonderful aspects of your personality. Through interacting with others, you will find that every person has a purpose in life and life itself has a purpose for all. Through caring and embracing each other in times of goodness and adversity, you will discover that you are never alone throughout your physical life journey.

The meeting and greeting of souls both in your world as well as those entering the earth plane through birth can feel very natural for the human experience. Often a rush of energy will penetrate throughout the spine in the knowing that good times are ahead and getting to know one another will be a joy. Sometimes you may feel a little impatient and wish to embrace all parts of the new soul entering your life.

It is important that you allow your relationship with other souls to unfold naturally. If you begin to place pressure on one another to be a certain person or conduct specific actions then the soul blending will no longer be a joy. Your spirits are interacting on the feelings of expectation, which can result in an eventual loss of the energy exchange.

Throughout your life there will be times when you feel that you have lost a connection with some souls. Gradually over time you may no longer feel the need to contact them and you may not be able to recognise the day when this process began. The pulling away from one another can be a natural progression for both of you identifying "who you are".

There is often a misinterpretation of people meeting and greeting one another and true soul mate connection. A deep soul connection does not mean that you need to spend your entire physical life with this person. In many cases, soul mates come together to teach one another various lessons throughout their journey. There is the hope that you will activate certain aspects of your personality in the further discovery of "who you are".

Do not place physical world belief systems on your soul interactions with one another. If you are bound by institutional laws of marriage, this does not mean that you cannot care for another soul of the opposite or same sex on an emotional and spiritual level. Your spirit does not understand limitations on love so therefore feelings of guilt and remorse for caring for another soul are unnecessary.

Allow yourself the opportunity to meet and interact with all walks of life including the plant and animal kingdoms. Extend your greetings to various races and religions in the hope that they will provide you with further insights into the psyche and living of the human race. It is this outlook that you will embrace along your own path of self-discovery that will allow you to further identify "who you are" through the essence of truth.

Grief

When one speaks of grief, an association of death and despair is often identified as part of the process. Physical death of a person may not be the circumstance but the death or the closing of a certain situation can leave a soul feeling some form of loss. This void in someone can be heartfelt especially when great levels of love were experienced before.

It is only through love that true grief can be felt. You cannot feel the hurt and pain of loss if you have never identified a gain in your life. This addition to your quality of life was something that you recognised previously and perhaps at times took for granted. In the moment of losing it in physical form, an instant feeling of gratitude is identified.

A part of "who you are" always resonates with the similarities or bonds in the bringing together of souls. The initial connection to another soul is something that is never forgotten. The person may not have exited from the earth plane through death however may no longer be a part of your everyday life.

Perhaps one of the strongest emotions tied with grief is loneliness. Humans operate their lives through forms of habit that determine daily activities and interests. These behavioural patterns are susceptible to vulnerability when drastic unexpected changes occur in one's life. Swift changes in the physical world can bring about feelings of imbalance causing the soul to sometimes respond in an irrational manner.

When a disconnection or loss of contact occurs between souls, self-destructive aspects of the personality can manifest over time. A deep soul connection can bring about unwanted feelings of anger, resentment and guilt that is unhealthy for the person experiencing grief. This can result in the use of drugs, alcohol or other forms of medication to relieve the pain.

Pain is something that is temporary but can feel eternal. The mind can produce signals in the brain indicating that the pain is worsening or manage to block it out completely depending on the mindset of the individual. Depression and illness can create a reality that life is not worth pursuing, as days and nights are occupied with feelings of misery.

Coming to terms with truth is a very important part of the grieving process. Even those passing through physical illness must process the various stages of grief either prior or during their transition to the spirit world. The stages of Denial, Anger, Bargaining, Depression and Acceptance can all be experienced at different levels and varying intensity.

It is important that the discussion of truth by all parties involved in the grieving process is encouraged.

Sharing your emotions and feelings can not only heal you, it can provide others with another perspective on life as well. This greater viewpoint of individual life plans can be very inspiring when recognition of soul growth is identified in everyone.

Always remember that you are never alone in your experiences. Another soul somewhere has been through very similar or almost identical circumstances as you and they have all survived this even through physical death. Once you recognise that this pain is only temporary and your soul is everlasting and ever-changing, your life will become more dynamic and less static throughout progression.

Growth

Like a fish that comes to the surface and breathes in air, a growth spurt within you is very similar in characteristics. There is a moment of realisation that one is outside their normal everyday conditions, but there is also a rush of energy knowing that limitations have been pushed beyond everyday thoughts. It is these moments in life that you will embrace in the afterlife as being moments of complete joy.

Throughout their earthly lives, most human beings find themselves believing their minds and bodies have not extended to their full capacity. A part of the spirit is ignited but there is no air in the atmosphere to fuel the flame. There can be a reliance of others around you to motivate your actions or inform you of your own possibilities. Very few people actually ask themselves what they would like to achieve in their lifetime and go ahead without seeking approval from others.

Growth is simply a term that is used to describe the progression of a thought, action or object from one time or place to another. It is a measurement of relativity and is normally judged on the viewpoint of the observer at any one point in time. This viewpoint of course is influenced by expectations and belief systems based on the initial growth stick firmly staked into the ground. Without warning, this growth stick can be moved, leaving souls feeling as though no progression has been made at all.

From time to time throughout your earthly lives, it is important that you embrace your growth chart on all levels: physically, mentally and spiritually. Stop every now and then and see how far you have progressed recently. Embrace that you are an ever-changing soul experiencing life through your own experiences and the experiences of others. Every part of you is worth exploring and the expansion of "who you are" will be a joy for all to see.

On children's birthdays, reflect on how far they have grown, not only physically but mentally as well. Learning new methods of exploring the arts, sports, mathematics and literature can be fun for many children and the simplest of projects given to a child can be the most rewarding. In a non-competitive environment, a child will feel as though they have achieved the unachievable, and normally will share these achievements with adults in the form of gifts given.

If you wish to explore how far you have progressed in your current life, simply observe yourself on your own birthday and embrace the gifts of "who you are". Spend time in a relaxed state and attempt to reflect on the magic moments you have experienced in your younger years. Ask yourself what made you happy throughout those milestones. Attempt to identify the key flames that ignited your spirit in those times of joy and peace.

Once you identify these, it is simple for you to continue to activate these bursts of light in anything you attempt to do in life. If being a child is required at times, then so be it. The most creative and influential projects in the world have been inspired under the guidance of the inner child. The inner child does not understand limitations, stakes placed into the ground or what is deemed to be acceptable or realistic in your lifetime. Growth is something that can never be measured in the physical world as the soul is ever-changing with an ever-changing universe of expansion and creativity.

Guides

True guidance of a soul involves understanding the universal laws of free will and choice. When one soul attempts to guide another through love, they will encourage the person to make choices that are of the highest good in their current life journey. A guide does not make choices for another soul but rather places certain circumstances, opportunities and possibilities that would seem to be favourable for their decision-making processes.

Guidance is given daily to human beings by those living in the physical and the spirit world. So much of the population may only see guidance as coming from the higher realms when a lot of opportunities are placed by living people. The belief that assistance must be given first by a higher force limits your mind's ability to identify true guidance when it's created in the first place.

If a person living a life in the physical world is strongly connected to "who you are", their ability to be a guide for the higher intent of your life would be of greater probability. Their natural bonding to their own spirit will operate in a similar manner when working with the requirements of your own soul. These people will naturally inspire you in a way that your own spirit will speak to you which can be the greatest guidance any soul should ever seek.

The speaking of your own spirit to your lower human ego is a wonderful gift that every person should embrace. Your own spirit has survived many incarnations of life and understands its purpose as to why it has chosen to return for another physical existence. Your spirit will give you a gut feeling of what is the correct path and too often this guidance is missed or disregarded altogether.

Why should your own spirit be less worthy in guiding your life than the spirit of other entities? It is very difficult to listen to the words of another spirit if you are not able to silence your own mind and allow your own spirit to come forward. Only your spirit has the ability to be constantly connected to your physical body with the possibility of being available for guidance on a day-to-day basis.

There can be the worshipping of spirit entities in higher realms in the hope of providing you with answers on your life path. These spirit entities play a major role in shifting the mass consciousness of the earth plane but they are not responsible for making life-changing decisions on your current path. Their quest is to inspire you to the extent that your soul comes forward in the hope of being recognised in "who you are".

Once you understand "who you are" then guidance from the higher part of yourself will filter through to your physical existence and a feeling of alignment will be experienced in your life. The natural guidance that has always been with you throughout your earthly life will become a new best friend once again. Continue to listen to this greatest guide that has re-entered your life.

Guilt

When your life is travelling along a path of bliss, there can be a level of underlying guilt that enters your mind with lower level thoughts and feelings. You may begin to believe that you are not worthy of such happiness in your life and other less fortunate souls are suffering with limited assistance. This can leave you in a state of anxiety and possibly, depression at times.

It is important to understand that greater levels of energy through exchange can and will assist you and others. If you decide to lower your vibration through self-inflicted guilty feelings, you are no longer inspiring "who you are" or those around you. Your inner being will eventually suffer through lack of self-love and limited acceptance of yourself and other souls.

Many people say that others can make them feel guilty. Most of the time these surrounding people are not inflicting those thoughts onto you but rather you are creating a projection in your own mind of what your own thoughts are about yourself. Your personality may be one of outer blame instead of inner self-reflection, causing a struggle between your spirit and human ego throughout your earthly experience.

The death of a loved one can create a reality that differs greatly between the two worlds. If someone was of a controlling nature in their physical life, upon passing into the spirit world there would be a realisation that this type of behaviour in their new life is no longer necessary. However, those who have been left behind on the earth plane may continue to believe that those personalities are observing and criticizing their lives, causing further feelings of guilt and blame to occur.

The human mind is powerful in creating thoughts and feelings within itself and then projecting these as owned by outside souls. This is very common in times of grief when questions were never answered, or outstanding issues were not resolved before death. This can leave the person feeling they are responsible for the final chapter of another person's life on earth.

Once a soul moves into the spirit world for a new life, their viewpoint of priorities will quickly change. Their reliance on earthly world matters is no longer necessary and a deep reflection of love for oneself as well as others will occur throughout their life review. The person will come to the realisation that they are much more than a physical body and perhaps could have interacted and connected more greatly with humanity.

It is easy for those left behind on the earth plane to place these souls in a higher order due to their physical death. The personality of a person does not change upon transition to their new life but rather their awareness expands through the realisation of "who they are". This does not mean they do not have further expansion ahead of them, they will continue to progress through new learning just like all souls do in the physical world.

Projecting thoughts of guilt onto yourself and those living in the spirit world achieves no healing at all. It simply lowers the vibration of all of those connected to the thoughts, resulting in further feelings of self-blame and hurt. Attempt to send loving and positive thoughts to those in both worlds in the hope that a shift in mindset will occur.

Happiness

When you understand that your thoughts contribute to your reality, you will then see that much of your happiness lies in your own hands. The perception of the life you live today is important in how you will experience joy and love tomorrow. Even under the most tragic of circumstances, attempt to see the light and memories you experienced with those that you have cared deeply for and loved in the past and present.

If you place high expectations on yourself, you are constantly thinking of how to achieve certain goals in specific time frames. This unnecessary pressure can leave you feeling stressed and insufficient in the creation of new thoughts and ideas. The drive and enthusiasm that originally provided you with the inspiration may be lost in the translation of fear.

Understand that your life is to be enjoyed by you and those who are a part of your daily life. If you are feeling happy and joyful, share this wonderful energy with others. Those who are experiencing sadness or depression will be naturally uplifted through your presence without the need for words to be spoken.

Laughter is very healthy for the mind, body and spirit and it is important that you do not take yourself or others too seriously all the time. Humour can open the heart and mind in ways that otherwise may never have been experienced. Telling a joke or funny story can leave a person with feelings of euphoria that can last for the rest of the day. This energy is contagious for those who find themselves in such comfort.

If you wish to experience happiness in your life, then surround yourself with souls who entertain these feelings. Being constantly suppressed by others is not a healthy way to discover "who you are". Allow yourself to experience moments of self-acceptance and love by indulging in your own space and energy at times. This does not mean engaging in physical life activities, it simply requires silencing of your own mind.

If you find that your thoughts are constantly flowing through your mind without a break then give yourself permission to slow these down or stop them completely. This of course does require a discipline that can be trained over a period of time. If you say to your own soul, in your own mind, that you are worthy of happiness and peace, you will begin to believe in "who you are" which can then settle your mind.

Once you know and understand that a soul is part of the mind, you will begin to see that a positive mindset can provide self-worth comments in your daily thoughts. By treating yourself as a spirit instead of a body you will accept that you are a spiritual being here for a physical experience and not a physical person having an occasional spiritual awakening.

Happiness is what every soul wishes to experience. Whether or not one resides on the earth plane or in another realm of life, it is the expression of oneself in its greatest form. This provides the joy and love within the spirit. Each and every one of you deserves these wonderful feelings and by shifting your mindset, you will soon realise that it is accessible by those who are willing to surrender to "who they are".

Healing

Across the world, different forms of healing are practised every day. Some may consider natural Eastern methods to be of a greater healing nature then those of the Western parts of the world. However, in essence all methods have the potential to provide favourable results. Limiting yourself to a particular method based on origin limits your capability to heal on many levels.

Healing can be provided to the mind, body and spirit. By simply listening to someone who is stressed or requiring some guidance, it can give tremendous support for the soul seeking their own answers. Often when someone talks to another person they find themselves answering their own questions that they may have struggled with for some time.

The settling of the human mind can be achieved through outward support of others or inward projection of yourself through meditation. By allowing your soul to express itself openly and honestly in a verbal or more silent manner, it has the capability to still the mind like a wave that crashes on the sand. These moments of breaking the restlessness in the mind can provide revelations of "who you are".

Keeping the mind active through greater learning is also a form of healing. By focusing your energy on matters outside of yourself, it allows you to see the bigger picture of life which motivates you to actively become a part of it. Over time you will begin to open your mind to new possibilities, which can reduce judgement of yourself and others in the path of self-discovery.

The human body has a remarkable capability of responding well to positive forms of energy. By rebalancing certain chemicals in the body, it has automatic functions of reproducing substances that previously may have been lost or imbalanced. Oxygen and water are vital elements of the human body and should be supplemented on a daily basis. Breathing in fresh air with no pollutants and drinking sanitised water is of great importance as well.

Restoration of the body muscles and tissues through exercise is also an important form of healing. Having an understanding of your physical limits according to your body size is critical when deciding what you will place yourself through. Enhancing your size through exercise is not harmful unless you introduce chemicals and substances that are foreign to the normal reproductive dosages of your body.

Spiritual healing can play a very important role in the maintenance of your mind, body and spirit. Meditation can relax and blend all three levels and provide discipline in your life towards synchronicity. This does not mean that you need to sit still and listen to certain tones of music to connect and heal yourself. Meditation and relaxation can be done in the form of anything you enjoy in life including walking, gardening, swimming, painting, listening to your favourite music or even cooking.

As long as your soul has the capability of recognising that it needs to re-balance itself, it then has the ability to self-heal on many levels. Sending prayers to both yourself and others is a very powerful form of healing. Positive thoughts can be sent and received if those connected through prayer are open to those rays of light. The gifts of healing energy can then filter through the spirit body and positively affect the functions of the physical body.

There are no limits to the healing possibilities that are sent and received. The sending of loving thoughts in the mental fields can also be supplemented with hands-on healing with the physical body. Both these methods can be complimentary to one another with different energies playing varying roles. A simple prayer to yourself or another soul does not require training, only positive and re-enforcing thoughts of love and compassion are required.

Health

Perhaps one of the greatest subject matters to be raised to the spirit world is that of health. Many feel as though they do not currently have the answers in maintaining a vibrant mind, body and spirit and attempt to seek the guidance of others outside of "who you are". No soul knows your mental, physical and spiritual wellbeing more than you. The art of listening to oneself is the key to maintaining good health.

Health is not something that can be broken down into the three distinctive categories of mind, body and spirit. It is holistic and every day you are constantly connecting to levels within this blend. These aspects of oneself are interconnected through energy. Through lack of vibrancy in one or more areas, ill-health can result.

Unfortunately the human race has a tendency to operate on a more reactive basis rather than working in a proactive manner. The ill-health of the planet and mistreatment of Mother Earth is a prime example of failing to recognise that continued exploitation of energy without renewable resources only results in further exhaustion.

The same also applies to individual human health. Very few people take the time to examine and reassess their health on a continued basis, including seeking guidance and expertise from practitioners in mental, physical and spiritual areas. By ensuring that stress levels are reduced at home and at work, the possibilities of mental illness would decline significantly if awareness of early signs were known.

Only you know your stress limits in life and only you are aware of your emotions and moods on a constant basis. If you find that you have a self-denial type of personality, simply diarise your feelings openly and honestly. This can provide greater clarity into the areas that require nurturing in your life and upon reflection over time you can examine the peaks or troughs in behaviour.

It is important that you do not over-analyse how you feel. The human ego can attempt to mask the truth of your initial thoughts and emotions. Upon observing your expressions in life, you may find patterns arising of a similar nature. The types of people who surround you, certain chemicals in your body that change due to hormones, diet or life cycles and the environment you live in can cause dramatic changes in your mental, physical and spiritual wellbeing.

The human body is a very important vessel for your existence on the earth plane. In order to live a life on earth, you require a physical instrument. It does not matter how brilliant your mind may be or how vibrant your spirit is, you still need to have a body to reside in that vibrates at the frequency of life on earth. The physical world is a world of matter so you will require a material body in order to survive.

A lot of people overwork the mind intellectually or meditate for hours in an attempt to raise their vibration, but all of this does not serve a purpose on earth without a physical existence of some form. Do not forget that you are having a physical life as well as a mental and spiritual one, and it is important that you eat and exercise correctly in your life to maintain a balance as well.

Home

It is often said that home is where the heart is. The true meaning behind this implies that the physical structure of the house does not provide warmth, comfort and fond memories. It is the embracing of the souls within that residence that brings about a sense of peace for those entering the space. It is a reminder of "who you are" in a non-judgemental environment.

Upon entering this space, there can be memories of friends and relatives that have since passed over but their presence is still strong. Photos of both the living and deceased provide you with a knowingness that you are loved and cared for by many who accepted most or all aspects of your personality. Coming home to this place provides you with gratitude of how good your life has been at certain points in time.

Attachments to your home are not just based on the beauty of the structure and its belongings. When homes are lost through forces of nature, it leaves feelings of abandonment, as the connection to the vibrations of energies within the place may feel like they are gone forever. It is important to remember that these bonds of love can be re-created in another space if you open your heart and mind beyond the physical limitations.

When you eventually pass over, the home you will create in the spirit world will more than likely be a replica of the places where you had your fondest memories here on earth. If there are many places that you enjoyed, then your home can be a combination of all those spaces together. There are no limits to the environment you choose to create in your own reality.

When a person is away from their familiar space for lengthy periods of times they can feel "homesick". The connection they have with other people either in or around the residence can be stronger whilst physically disconnected, which can bring about wonderful feelings of love and gratitude. The bonding of souls can be reassessed through reflection which can strengthen relationships even more in the future.

When a person grows older in life and needs to be placed in a residence of care, it is important that there are belongings around them that create a heartfelt environment. The scent of flowers, photo frames with memories or even a picture from their previous home can make them feel comfortable in times of disorientation or loneliness.

When considering a place of residence to call your home, always feel the energy when entering the space. Your initial thoughts and feelings are important in ensuring that your soul experiences the correct environment for your journey. Cleansing the area with positive energy, music or other spiritual methods prevents you from absorbing residual energy from previous inhabitants.

Always have gratitude for the shelter that your home provides to you on a day-to-day basis. Nurture and care for any plants or animals that are part of the natural environment you live in. Have a respectful and positive relationship with your neighbours. This can then flow onto the greater community, creating peace and harmony for humanity at large.

Hope

Those who are more hopeful in life seem to live a much happier existence than those who are not. Are these underlying thoughts more than just wishful thinking? Or is there a direct correlation between the mindset of oneself and the reality of the result of this positive mindset? If one is more hopeful in life then there is a greater ability for their energy levels to rise above the current physical vibration that exists.

If you are more hopeful in life then you are reaching out to achieve or obtain something greater than the current reality you reside in. Is this not just an extension of the creation process? If everything in the universe is first created with a thought, then any wishful thinking is merely only considered to be a wish until the universe grants the request into physical matter.

The universe does not judge these requests. In time there is no reason why these positive thoughts cannot be granted on the earth plane in the perfect time and space. The reason why time and space are of importance is that the request may be fulfilling the purpose of many souls all interconnected on the universal grid of light. This connectivity or oneness is what enables the human spirit to truly understand the meaning of hope.

It is through the testing times of mass crisis that the human spirit has the ability to raise itself above self-pity and have gratitude for all that it experiences right now. The spirit sees that other souls are perhaps worse off and considers them not to be separate from itself. The disconnection of the human spirit will no longer be felt amongst the community, allowing the creation process to begin once more through positive connectivity.

Sometimes it can take a major crisis in one's life, or to witness an incident in someone else's life, to feel the gratitude and hope on another level. Most of the time a shift in the mindset is required at some level for this rise to occur. Once the spirit knows that nothing can ever harm it, including physical death, there is always hope that the human experience can only become more insightful for the evolving soul.

You do not always need to share your hopes and desires with other people. You only need to be truthful to yourself with these requests. Every individual deserves the possibility to extend themselves to higher ground on all levels of the mind, body and spirit. Once you have mastered certain aspects of this natural extension of "who you are" then you can assist the less fortunate who do not see themselves as creators of the universe.

Humanity

One of the greatest misconceptions any human being can have is that they are alone in life. Humanity does not operate on a level of separation and is always bonded by the spirit of connectivity through unity. Unfortunately it is often through adversity that people realise they are a part of something far greater than themselves.

When a disaster or tragic circumstance occurs amongst a community, the human spirit is tested on many levels. Resources may be limited causing panic amongst those who are concerned about their physical welfare and survival. Others will rely on their faith and beliefs to get them through the unknown periods whilst some may have no feelings or emotions at all towards the situation at hand.

Regardless of age, financial status, beliefs or race, people can be forced to come together through unfortunate events. An immediate removal of judgements created by the human ego allows everyone to accept one another on a more spiritual level. There is an understanding that human beings are more common than different to one another and facing similar struggles throughout their lives.

Everyday issues such as work, relationships, health and love are common amongst most people in different communities. The levels and ways of dealing with the issues may vary but the underlying emotional and physical acceptance will be almost the same. The knowing of "who you are" is an important factor in coming to terms with the struggles and eventually embracing the outcome.

When meeting someone for the first time, your initial thoughts and judgements will be very much dependent upon your own belief systems of what you consider to be acceptable in a society. When this society changes dramatically for reasons outside of your control, reassessment of "who you are" is immediately required.

Filters that may have blocked your view will soon expose the truth, allowing you to see things more widely. You will be drawn to the commonalities in people around you rather than the differences, which will give you more energy to accept yourself and others. You may suddenly be drawn to certain people that were not considered to be friends, colleagues or partners in the past.

Trust and truth amongst humanity is much stronger when the human ego is forced to break down the barriers and invite others into their lives. Through dependency on the physical, emotional, mental and spiritual levels within the community, aspects of your personality will be activated that may have remained dormant throughout your life. You may feel more compassion and understanding for people that you didn't previously consider to be in need of assistance.

Through forced changes that occur within the human race, people often cannot return to the lives they knew before. Deeper soul connections have been established and there seems to be a wanting to continue to take care of one another in the future. Individual self-gain becomes of less importance with a sense of being part of something far greater than "who you are".

Those who are observing this change in behaviour can also be emotionally and spiritually affected. They may be willing to give up something of their own to assist those in need as they are now able to place themselves into the shoes of others. This knowingness that humanity is connected on a deeper level can bring about the power of change for a more peaceful planet for all to experience.

Humour

One of the greatest gifts you can give to yourself is the ability to laugh. When one takes their life so seriously, it closes down the mind in such a way that new possibilities and opportunities can be missed due to high expectations and judgements. Once you stop judging yourself, you will embrace the diversity of life surrounding you even more.

If life was meant to be so serious then what would be the purpose of it all? What would you learn and experience in your life if you already knew and controlled the outcome of the many possibilities at hand? Once you understand that the journey itself is of importance and not the actual temporary outcome then you will begin to enjoy the wonders of life itself.

Life is not meant to be smooth, otherwise you would never discover "who you are" through both adversity and joy. In the darker moments of your life, you may remember instances where comments were made with humour that others may have considered to be inappropriate. These responses are your own way of expressing your feelings and emotions on the situations that confront you.

Throughout the life cycles of birth and death, much humour is witnessed. Funerals can carry a sense of laughter, especially in the moments of remembering past events and heartfelt moments. After one passes into the spirit world, very little thought is given to the struggles in life they may have experienced, but rather the joys and wonderful incidents that touched people's hearts.

It is often surprising to witness from the spirit world, the shock that some people feel when they realise that those grieving for them actually cared about them in their own way. The observation of family, work colleagues, ex-partners or even distant friends and relatives attending a funeral service and commenting on one's experiences, with humour, is a realisation in itself that life should not be taken too seriously.

Some souls may feel that certain people did not like them in the physical world when in fact they did not mind their company at all. Perhaps these people were not interested in the career, material gain or wealth, religious or political points of view of the person in passing, but they could see the greater humour and joy in their personalities whilst in their physical presence.

If a person is seeking acceptance of themselves by others based on their physical world attributes, then it is very difficult to see who enjoys the actual company of their spirit. The greatest realisation of this connectivity of souls is through humour, joy and love. Once you allow yourself to express this openly, you are then able to identify and express this in a sharing and giving way to other people.

Humour is one of the greatest medicines that the mind, body and spirit can give to itself and others, especially when love and joy are lacking in one's life.

The opening of the heart and lungs through laughter allows more oxygen to flow through your vessel giving your life-force a further opportunity to ignite. This ignition is highly contagious and in time you may find even strangers attracted to your company.

There is no punishment for laughter, so why would the human race feel a lack of need to embrace it? If it is a natural part of "who you are" then allow yourself to express it openly. If the laughing of yourself and others does not carry judgement, then the benefits of this wonderful gift can be very surprising for yourself and each other.

Hurt

When one exposes themselves to certain experiences in life, there is always the possibility that some form of hurt or pain is felt on a deeper soul level. This hurt and pain normally requires emotional and spiritual reflection of the situation at hand in an attempt to forgive those involved, including oneself. The feeling of abandonment can be overwhelming throughout these times, since the person may be drawn towards the need to disconnect from those around them in life.

Pain can be viewed as something that is more measurable than hurt. Being hurt by someone normally follows a cumulative process of hurt that has been experienced in other situations of similar nature. Past relationships are an example of allowing oneself to hold onto feelings and emotions of anger or frustration that may have resulted from people who are no longer a part of your current life.

The feelings of hurt can cause tolerance levels to reduce significantly. In some situations this can result in decisions being made to avoid certain people and circumstances altogether. High levels of judgement can then become a part of your personality causing further disconnection as others choose not to be in your present company.

General statements can be made at times when the topic is not even of relevance. Placing people in certain categories of betrayal and mistrust will limit your possibilities of further healing. New energy and vibrancy is always required for your soul to progress further in life. By cutting out these new possibilities and souls coming into your life, you are only hurting yourself even more.

If you observe someone who is hurting, attempt to listen without judgement. Allow yourself to be placed in their shoes and ask yourself what you would have done in their situation. If you believe that you could address the situation in a more positive and meaningful manner then attempt to do so if you feel that it will provide clarity for the person at hand.

Normally, when you speak to someone in the third person, they may be less defensive about the nature of your opinions. Perhaps you could use an example of a situation similar to the one that they are discussing with you. Attempt to provide various viewpoints from all parties involved in a manner that allows the other person to understand.

Raising another person's awareness of "who you are" can be very powerful in the healing process of hurt. Encouraging them to let go of the past opens new avenues and doorways that may otherwise have not been recognised in the future. Listening to them with empathy and compassion can be a wonderful gift as you learn more about human behaviour and the reasoning behind certain actions.

Those who are hurting deeply mostly just want to be heard and understood by others who are open enough to listen to their story. You do not necessarily need to have similar circumstances to be respected as a listener, but rather an open heart and mind filled with compassion and empathy for others.

Identity

Coming to terms with "who you are" is perhaps one of the greatest joys in life. This road is not something that can be taken on your own but rather requires passengers along the way. Each and every person you interact with will activate a certain aspect of your individual personality. This gift is something that should not be taken for granted but rather embraced in your daily lives.

Every person attempts to search for their own individuality and identity in life. They wish to pursue the uniqueness within themselves in the hope that their light can shine through and be noticed by others. However it is important to realise that your true identity can only be realised through the greater connectivity and unity of humanity.

Activation of varying degrees of your psyche provides a foundation for getting to know "who you are". Letting go of past thoughts and actions are also required in the opening of new doorways in your life. Different players will provide you with insights that perhaps you previously never considered as a possibility. This can inspire you to reach higher in your achievements and have further gratitude for your current life.

Every individual carries within their own soul wonderful gifts to be shared with many people. Sometimes these wonders are not discovered until another person takes an interest in this part of "who you are". Acceptance and love from others can lead your life into the direction that it was meant to flow in your current physical existence.

It is important that you recognise the individuality of all people of different races and religions. The underlying commonality of truth stems from the unity of humanity on a deeper level. If everyone believed that all souls deserve to be treated with equality, than understanding of oneself would be transparent for all who are willing to see.

Life itself would not carry the joys and exciting moments without the individuality of the human race.

Often a soul can make another person laugh at the simplest joke by allowing them to see things from another perspective. The gift of one's identity is the ability to project another viewpoint based on their own past experiences and belief systems.

When a person falls deeply in love with another person, there can be the feelings of combining both identities into one. This is the result of blending one another's energies in such a manner that separation of the souls seems impossible. This complete acceptance of "who you are" has the ability to extend amongst other people in your life.

Often when a person is in a happy and fulfilling relationship they seem to be more tolerant to individual behaviours in their life. They can be less judgemental as they have learnt to accept their own traits as well as someone else's. They have embraced the good with what they consider to be the bad and the eclipse of the dark and light brings about a unity in an area of middle ground. This is where individualism begins to merge with the greater consciousness of humanity on the quest of identifying "who you are".

Individuality

The path of self-discovery in "who you are" involves searching within the individual aspects of your own self as well as others. Coming to terms with your true identity cannot be done alone, as life itself is not meant to be a journey of sole enlightenment. Each and every one of you is born with gifts that are meant to be shared with other people. Learning to embrace those individual treasures is one of the greatest achievements you will ever experience in this lifetime.

The search for "who you are" is also accomplished through the discovery of "who you are" not. Coming to terms with both the light and dark aspects of personalities is important in identifying your own light within. It is often through hurt, pain and suffering that a soul will stand true in their belief as to what is considered to be right or wrong for their own current existence.

What may have been considered to be acceptable action undertaken by them or others in the past may no longer be embraced. Through experience, one is able to place themselves into the shoes of others and see the effect of an individual action on the whole of other people's lives. This greater effect allows the soul to understand on a spiritual level that even though they may be of individual personality, connectivity automatically causes a bigger impact to all.

This concept of connectivity of souls is not always something that is conscious. When one personality decides to undertake a certain action, the impact it has on either the planet and/or its inhabitants is not always considered. Whether or not this is indirect contamination of minds or bodies through methods such as media or pollution, a greater viewpoint is not always naturally taken.

Society continually strives to create similarities through the promotion of fashion and marketing. It seems however they are not always willing to embrace the balance of individuality that also exists between souls. The acceptance of different shapes, sizes and sexuality is important when attempting to activate equality in the human life existence.

Over-promotion and glorification of certain celebrity personalities is not healthy for any society. Not only does it create an idea of perfection in many people's minds, it also creates a mindset of self-destruction for the individual celebrity, seeking to be imperfect on a deeper level. Constant attacking by media that initially created the identity, results in a fabrication of one's personality causing a rebelling in "who they are".

It seems that the initial worshipping of individual personalities is activated by the feelings in others that they hope to achieve this perception of "who they are" in life. Over time this perception can change according to expectations and beliefs which can then manifest into false hope and untruths. The loss of reality that these people are also human along a path of self-discovery can leave many with the feeling of disappointment and deception when the truth is finally revealed.

When embracing individual aspects of personalities, attempt to see the truth and love within both yourself and others. Only then can you truly see "who you are". Attempt to activate parts of yourself that may have remained dormant within your current life. Self-pity and lack of self-worth are not healthy role models throughout this journey. Embrace all of those who surround your life with the knowing that every individual is part of the greater whole through connectivity in the web of life.

Innocence

When a baby is born into the physical world, its mind has ventured from a world of purer and clearer thoughts. Upon entering the atmosphere of the earth plane, the density of matter imposes heavier sensations, preparing the spirit for a journey of seeking truth once again. The loss of innocence on the road of self-discovery will open new avenues and doorways.

As the fear of the unknown lies behind those doors, the human ego begins to examine the differences between what is real and what is not in its own reality. The untouched spirit will accept what is in front of them as truth and they will exert less effort attempting to change what was to what should be. Their eyes will be open to the possibility of obtaining enjoyment and love from other human beings.

This level of naivety and innocence is necessary for the earth plane to continue to exist at a vibration that encourages joy and happiness. These souls will bring together strangers who otherwise may have nothing in common throughout their physical existence. Children and animals are examples of this purity and should be treated and celebrated with respect by all souls who have the privilege to interact with them.

It is important that the human ego does not attempt to contaminate or harm these innocent souls when they open themselves up for kindness and forgiveness. Human nature has a way of impressing their little minds that certain thoughts and actions that are deemed favourable to their own human experience are not acceptable for others to be exposed to.

Constant reassessment of one's intention towards self and others is required in the discovery of "who you are". Never allow anyone else to tell you "who you are" or what you should be. Do not believe that your own mental, physical or emotional state is open for others to destroy or tarnish in any manner. Your innocence is something to be kept throughout your earthly journey so you can embrace life in its purest form.

If your innocence has been subjected to negative behaviour in the past then try and encourage it to come forward again. Attempt to take away your belief systems that no-one can be trusted and that all people act in the same way. If you were unable to shield yourself from negative thought patterns or behaviours before, then at least attempt to allow the positive mindset of your inner child to be entertained.

Ask yourself in your day-to-day lives why you engage in certain leisure activities. Is it to obtain a healthy physical state or to connect with other likeminded souls? But what if you did not need to have a purpose for the interaction? What would you do if it did not matter what you did? Would your soul find itself in a state of bliss, engaging in painting, drawing, singing, dancing, or just sitting with oneself?

If you feel the need to find that place inside of you that has been lost in the journey of life, observe the children and animals. Ask what it is that makes most of them so happy. Is it that they do not think in a cynical and polluted manner? Do they accept that not everyone is the same and we have the opportunity to embrace and encourage the similarities and differences in each other? Innocence is simply the removal of filters that are placed on the mind by the human ego.

Inspiration

When you feel inspired a part of "who you are" is activated which brings about a sense of inner peace. This boost in energy feeds your soul in a manner that gives you permission to surrender and trust in the path that is to follow. In these sudden moments of clarity, you may not have thought about the mechanics of bringing it together or why you need to follow it. You just know that the idea is something that you at least wish to pursue further.

It seems that these moments can provide you with joy in the knowing that there are always other ways that life can be experienced. You can contribute to these new ways of thinking by simply opening yourselves up to different possibilities and methods of thought processing. You do not necessarily need to be an expert in a particular field of study or even have skills in the topic of your inspiration.

Some of the greatest inspirations have come from observing the lives of others. Poetry, music and dance can be composed by interacting with the minds of fellow human beings who are affected by love, sadness, joy and other deep emotions felt in life. Once you know that you are all interconnected and share the same source of energy, this realisation can manifest into wonderful new experiences.

By understanding various races, religions and cultures across the earth plane, your ability to produce a variety of inspiring thoughts will be far greater than confining yourself to limited lifestyle patterns. Tasting and smelling the cuisines of the world can open your mind to different realities without even visiting the source destinations. You can place yourself where those essences of life were first inspired through the human senses.

A lot of people have wonderful concepts and designs that could help themselves and the rest of humanity. Their souls in these moments of inspiration know and feel that their contribution would be of heartfelt assistance. However, what occurs after these initial thoughts is the intrusion of the human ego through self-doubt, negative emotions and lack of self-love.

The ability to bring forward inspiration from the soul to the physical world requires stamina and persistence. If you are not affected by the human ego thoughts of your own mind then there is still a good possibility that others will attempt to take away your inspiration. It is important that you remember "who you are" and always understand that you are a powerful human being.

Throughout the process of assessment in the implementation of your inspiration, ensure that you align yourself with like-minded souls who have similar intentions to you. Never allow anyone to tell you that your input is less worthy than their feedback. Continue to believe in "who you are" and you will find that assistance will come in forms that you least expect.

Each and every one of you has the right to be inspired by your soul and create a wonderful reality in life. Regardless of your financial background, ideas can be brought forward into the world of matter with trust and surrender. Your ideas can be in a mental or emotional form to assist others in life through love and teaching. It may be a physical object that requires earthly energy to exist. Either way, you can succeed in anything you do by simply just believing in your soul's inspiration.

Intention

One of the major challenges that many face throughout their lifetime is the alignment of what is outwardly portrayed from the human ego and their underlying real thoughts and emotions stemming from this initial projection. The distortion of one's truth can be all-consuming for some people, resulting in large amounts of energy being required to maintain smoke and mirrors.

If one is truthful in "who they are" to begin with, life can be very simple for them and those around them. By merely accepting "who you are", the inward love you have for yourself will now flow through to others by simply giving the permission to show your real self.

Emotionally, you can express with truth how you feel about certain subjects of discussion and not wait for the acceptance of those beliefs from others. You will have an understanding that your truth may not always be someone else's truth but you will be open to new ways of thinking and possibilities that perhaps were not considered before.

If your intention is one to be of open heart and open mind, you will find that information that initially may have been rejected in your thoughts will begin to resonate with you on a deeper level. You will understand that every person around you has the opportunity to teach you something new and you also have the gift of bringing forward your own philosophy in the greater picture of life.

Intention is not something that can be taught or mastered through tools given to a person. Pure intention comes from the soul expressing itself only through the love of the self and of others. This love requires a deeper level of compassion and kindness that for some can only be expressed when they are exposed emotionally to a situation that forces them to re-evaluate their life.

Unfortunately, for most souls the assessment of one's intention is almost always shifted through a sudden self-reflection. A divorce in marriage, failed business, loss of a life or witnessing unlawful behaviour can bring about a large amount of guilt and frustration. The person knows on a deeper level that they could have risen above the occasion and extended themselves much further in the previous chapters of their lives now that they can observe them so remotely.

Your intentions cannot be changed consciously but rather a conscious observation of your intentions can change everything. Once you realise where your initial thoughts stem from, you can attempt to redirect them in a manner that questions the purpose of the actions to follow. If those actions are not meaningful to the greater good of humanity and its inhabitants then you can simply choose not to execute them.

Once you begin to take action on your actions, any initial selfish thoughts will begin to starve and there will be a hunger in your soul like never before. Your mind will open itself to new ideas and inspirations. Over time without realising it, your purer thoughts can take action. Minimum conscious intervention between thought and action will then result. This shortened time-frame does not allow the human ego to step in with an attempt to self-gain.

Without you even consciously being aware of it, your intention will move along the scale of a more selfless and servicing life rather than that of self-gain and self-indulgence. You can experience greater happiness, which is the purest intention any soul wishes to achieve. You may not be consciously aware that it was initiated through the greater connectivity in the web of life rather than just yourself as an individual spider creating your own reality.

Intuition

Intuition is simply the listening to one's soul through subtle feelings of knowingness. Being in tune with your own self is a sign that connectivity between mind, body and spirit is occurring. When all three are aligned, in these moments you will feel through the physical body, or hear thoughts in your own mind of what your spirit would like you to do. Listening to your own soul is the most important guidance you will receive in your current lifetime.

It is natural for the human race to depend on thoughts or actions of others around them in order to make their own decisions. These others can include individuals, organisations or institutions. This dependency on intelligence outside of oneself can be unhealthy if the responsibilities of actions taken thereafter are also placed on the other. Under such circumstances, very little listening of the soul is occurring which can result in disconnection on many levels.

Often in a society where high levels of political and economic power are in force, individuals can feel powerless to express "who they are" with freedom. This capturing of a soul's ability to think and feel for itself can contribute to high levels of violence and resentment in the long run. People may feel as though their creative abilities cannot be expressed and therefore shared with the greater population.

Life on earth was never meant to be full of so much regimentation that a soul no longer recognises "who they are" through individualism. Having the ability to share ideas and thoughts with one another opens the intuitive mind to possibilities that were perhaps not considered to be feasible. If restraints on the day-to-day physical and mental life do not exist, then the spirit will feel free to express itself through inspiration.

It is important that the mind and body are kept in a healthy state to ensure that the messages you receive from your spirit are of clarity. If you pollute your mind with negative thoughts or substance abuse, your own ego may disguise itself as intuition, when in fact paranoia and delusional thoughts are running through your mind. If these thoughts are not of a positive or inspirational nature, then simply ignore them.

Thoughts of warnings will give you an action to follow that will be for the greatest good of all involved.

These feelings and thoughts will have less personal judgement of yourself as well as others. Your intuition will not tell you that you or anyone else is unworthy. It will simply guide you not to engage in certain behaviour or actions and move on immediately from the situation.

It is important that common sense is used when seeking wisdom from other souls. If people do not live a life of healthy mind, body and spirit by empowering their own thoughts and actions, then it is impossible for them to provide wisdom to others. Those who work from a vibration of love, truth and happiness will live by example and inspire many to listen to their own soul intuition that has been given as part of your own birthright.

Jealousy

When one feels jealousy towards another, it often stems from underlying emotions of resentment. This can bring forward aspects of the personality that you or others may consider less favourable in nature. Over time, these emotions can build up to the extent where paranoia and delusional thoughts can cause a person to act in an irrational manner.

If you or someone else discovers a situation engulfed by jealousy, it is important to assess the underlying source of those emotions. The jealousy may not be directly attributable to the person at hand but rather the circumstances that currently exist in their life.

Economic, political or social status can largely influence the perception of one's reality by another person.

It is easy to place labels on people who seem to have all that the universe can offer them. They may not outwardly portray any difficult circumstances at all. This allows others to perceive them as objects who can handle jealous outbursts either consciously or unconsciously. Targeting the lives of other people gives humanity the excuse not to address the underlying issues in their own lives.

Jealousy occurs when another person has someone or something in their life that others feel is missing from their own life. If you are not happy with the appearance of your physical body, those negative thought forms can manifest into resentment towards others who are happy with their appearance. If your mental health status is drained, you may retaliate towards others who have a positive and uplifting outlook in life.

Whenever feelings of jealousy arise in your life, it is a great opportunity for you to reflect on your deeper emotions and intentions. You will often find that those feelings will link to underlying disappointments or regret that you could have had those people or circumstances as part of your own life.

The reality of the situation is that you did not attract this into your life as part of the greater plan. Once you accept that this was not to be, then you will move on from these unnecessary thoughts and focus your energy onto higher vibration living. Jealousy stems from the human ego wanting acceptance and fulfilment at the physical level.

True love does not carry with it emotions of jealousy. The spirit understands that nothing can ever come between souls and harm them. A disconnection and lack of fulfilment is not possible with unity and connectivity. Feelings of love for multiple souls are natural, and foreign to the emotions that are carried with control and jealousy.

The truth will always set you free when attempting to understand the connections between people. If someone is not physically attracted to you in this lifetime then the souls were never meant to engage in this experience. If someone else is connected to your partner on a more intelligent or emotional level than you then this is the purpose of their soul exchange.

Never allow others to attempt to control "who you are" and what aspects of your personality can shine. Certain parts of you will come forward depending on the souls who surround you in life. If you feel love and compassion for many people, this is a natural progression towards unity and oneness. Attempt to strive for greater connections and from this you will express and know "who you are" in this life.

Joy

When you are joyful about something in your life then your heart, mind and soul will be aligned at once. These are wonderful feelings, without the regrets of the past or worries of the future. You know that anything is possible in these moments where time seems to make no sense. The mind takes an observation point of view instead of overwhelming you with negative impressions.

If others around you in life are joyful, this can be highly contagious. Seeing the wonders of someone unfolding "who they are" can inspire you to step out of your comfort zone and into your own space. Normally when one is expressing their true self, these moments of joy become more frequent throughout their lives.

Embracing every part of yourself is one of the greatest gifts your soul can give and receive. Taking opportunities when they arise allows your experience to unfold without knowing the outcome. This unsureness of what lies ahead gives you the realisation that life is meant to be a journey of exploration filled with moments of both uncertainty and bliss.

Joyful and blissful states can be seen through the windows of the soul. Light beams from these areas like an automatic switch that has been turned on. The spirit comes forward in the hope that it will be recognised in its happiest state. This allows you and others to accept "who you are" on many levels, which provides an excellent foundation for more wonderful adventures in the future.

In times of sadness or doubt, try to focus on past experiences that have provided you with joy. Always ask yourself what the circumstances were that surrounded you in those moments. Did you experience joy with other souls or was it something that you engaged in by yourself? Was your physical environment different as well as your mental, spiritual and emotional foundations?

Pure joy can be seen through the eyes of children. They do not understand rules and obligations of not expressing oneself openly and honestly. Young people have a natural ability to take further risks than the older generation and from this they will normally experience greater moments of joy and wonder in their lives. These risks do not need to be harmful to their physical life but rather an inspiration to the human spirit.

What normally holds someone back from experiencing the wonders of joy is the fear of rejection of "who they are". Wanting to be accepted amongst a society can cause an individual to express certain traits and attributes that are deemed to be favourable by others. This can consume high levels of energy by placing further truthful reservations on expressing oneself. Let go of this fear and allow your soul to step out so you can engage in the joyful life that each and every one of you truly deserves.

Judgement

Judgement is a word that is used very little in conversation but seems to take action in the mind many times each day. Whether this judgement is of oneself or another there is no difference. Opinions of characteristics are reflections of a lack of fulfilment within the souls themselves.

Each and every soul should be viewed as perfect at any one point in time without the need to seek approval or opinions from others on "who they are". Attempting to place someone in a particular category based on financial, sexual, religious or racial preferences achieves nothing but a perfume of low vibration with an unfavourable smell of fear and ego in the air.

When you meet someone for the first time, it is natural for the human mind to categorise them automatically. You may not even be aware of this happening, but most of the time common words will flow in and out of your mind depending on the first attributes of the person you choose to recognise.

Recognition of someone is linked to the recognition of your own self. If you immediately judge someone to be overweight or financially less fortunate than you, these initial thoughts are underlying fears that you never wish to be judged by others as being "who you are".

It is impossible for the human mind not to judge in the physical world since the environment has been built on a material plane where ego is an instilled part of the human race itself. Judgements need to be made when making decisions in order to survive. These judgements may include those made by governments, organisations and institutions for the greater survival of the planet and its inhabitants, including the availability of food, shelter and water.

When do these necessary judgements of survival practices no longer serve the greater spirituality of life for humanity? When is it unacceptable to control the earth's resources for all its inhabitants? It is when decisions are made on allocation of resources to souls based on financial, sexual, race or religious belief systems. If the individuals making these decisions have strong beliefs in any one of these categories then the balance of resourcing may not be achievable, causing segregation and isolation for certain souls.

Those who have strong belief systems in any one of these categories may have been exposed to these judgements from an early age in life. Their parents or mentors may have influenced their decision-making processes. Intensive life experiences throughout their youth may have cemented certain thoughts in their minds. Either way, these influences make it difficult for the soul to open itself to new possibilities.

It is only when you embrace the lives of those around you that you can then accept your own self. Once you let go of the fears and judgements you place onto others then you can begin to become more relaxed with "who you are". Everyone around you will be a reflection of yourself. You can eventually accept every trait of your own personality by encouraging aspects of others to shine.

Kindness

Kindness can be felt from anyone, from a stranger who walks on the street to a loving partner in your own home. An act of kindness is to extend yourself to others in the hope that the compassion you provide them will allow their own soul to feel gratitude for their existence on earth. The knowing that someone else cares about you can shift your day from that of darker shade to one of purer light.

When someone extends themselves to you through kindness, a heartfelt response is felt amongst all souls involved. There is an instant boost of energy so natural to the human race that other souls witnessing this will experience the inspiration to follow. Knowing that you are all a part of something far greater can provide your mindset with a wider viewpoint and the ability to solve any problem that may surface.

Being kind to other human beings is not the only direction to channel your energy. It is important that you are kind to yourself as well as other living species on your planet including plants and animals. Kindness is based on feeling and any living form that can feel pain or love will be receptive to any act of kindness throughout its existence.

Kindness should be nurtured in all children at a very young age. Empathy and compassion towards others is of importance for the soul to truly understand themselves and their surrounding human beings. It is not something that can be taught but rather encouraged so the individual naturally develops their own style in the delivery of their acts.

Society often views an act of kindness to be something that aligns with the overall morals and values of the community. Donating to an institution or organisation may be viewed to be kind when in fact there may be an underlying financial reason for undertaking such an act. It is important that a society does not set parameters on what should be viewed as a kind act and what is of low moral significance.

Being kind to someone is not the act of taking away pain. This is greatly confused with the need to want to control a situation and remove what is considered to be unwanted. True kindness is accepting a situation, soul or any living thing for what it is and providing love and support without judgement. It does not attempt to change anything but rather warrant permission for changes if destiny allows this to be.

Rekindling relationships is an example of accepting one another and learning to live with less judgement than before. It is coming to terms with the fact that no-one needs to be controlled but simply supported in "who they are". Some aspects of the personality may not be accepted but other parts are worth embracing again with a need to reignite a part of your own self through the energy exchange.

Coming to terms with "who you are" and who others are in your life is the greatest kindness you can ever experience. Accepting that not everyone is the same can be rejoicing for all involved. Being kind is not something that you need to be conscious of but rather listen to your heart when guidance is required to assist others. You will know the words to speak at the right time and you will also know when not to speak.

Knowledge

Knowledge is something that should not be confused with the word information. Information is simply the passing of words that may not necessarily have included any form of fact, past experiences or valid viewpoints. Knowledge, on the other hand, is information that has been examined much further at a deeper and more emotional level and incorporates the greater minds of the collective rather than the individual.

To be knowledgeable in an area of expertise is considered to be a form of privilege. This privilege is something that normally should involve the gathering of information and examination of certain outcomes in the hope that future assessments provide better ways of doing things for the greater good of humanity and the planet. It is something that should be encouraged and shared with as many souls as possible.

Many consider that holding on to information is powerful when in fact the sharing of knowledge is even more powerful. True inspirational knowledge is tangible in the lives of those who understand its essence in every form. It resonates with the soul when they hear the words flowing through their own mind upon receiving them. The spirit ignites with sureness in itself that these words are of truth in their understanding of how life should be.

A true knowledgeable person will not limit themselves with titles of "who they are". Having letters after their name provides a recognition that information has indeed flowed through their minds perhaps more often than the average person but it does not guarantee clarity of the greater path for all. Someone researching a cure for a global health crisis should consider the thoughts and experience of others in different fields of expertise before concluding their assessment.

To examine something from information given without the holistic approach to cause and effect will only result in problems existing on many levels. To judge a certain viewpoint to be right or wrong without consideration of others is arrogant and ignorant. This closing down of the mind does not encourage further wisdom and knowledge to flow from the greater collective minds.

In past times on the earth plane, knowledge was passed down through stories and parables that were easy for the people listening to understand. The hearing or reading of these words would resonate through the soul simply by placing the person into the experience themselves without ever actually being a part of the script in the first place. This can be a very powerful tool in the learning for the progression of the human soul.

When knowledge is passed through various minds, it is important to realise that filters will limit what has been given and received, causing one's perspective of truth to ultimately change. The more closed the mind of the individual giving and receiving the information, the wider the filter sorting through the information based on their own beliefs and experiences. These beliefs can range in intensity through religious, political and social viewpoints.

If knowledge is passed down to you from your own or another mind, always attempt to document or record these words before you examine them more closely. What you will find is that your own ego may disregard some of it immediately. However, in time through your own experiences or the observation of others you may find that your perspective on the situation may change with your dynamic viewpoints.

Leadership

It is natural for the human race to follow some form of leadership within society. Whether this leadership stems from large governments or tribal leaders, leadership is inevitable in any cultural experience. There is always some form of ownership placed on a spokesperson in the hope that the greater good of humanity will be achieved.

In most cases this spokesperson has been assigned to their position of power through the free will and choice of the masses. Either through a voting system or genetic trait of acceptance, the soul chosen to make impacting decisions for the group has an understanding on some level that they must attempt to meet the needs of the group at large. It is important at all times that the leader is aware of the reason why they were given such a position in the first place.

True leadership involves the ability to assess all circumstances and parties involved and attempt to make decisions based on fairness and equality. It should involve constant self-reflection and self-awareness of the role given. If a diversion in the feeling of the initial intention does occur, then a correction in leadership is required.

When one chooses to take on any role of leadership, it carries with it a high level of responsibility. It requires the soul to constantly attempt to achieve balance in the flow of energy between all parties involved. It also involves the ability to assess the greater impact of decisions that are made outside of the parties directly involved.

Education of oneself as a leader is very important. A closed-minded leader is unhealthy for decision making processes as new ideas and innovations are available in an ever-changing manner. Believing that one person has all the answers is ignorant to the fact that all human beings have the ability to think for themselves and contribute to society as a whole.

A true leader will take onboard feedback from the greater group in the hope that new processes of implementation can be achieved. There is always room for improvement and the ignition of souls can bring about inspiration. Those of open heart and open mind will always bring forward positive thoughts and feelings to be shared amongst those who are willing to listen.

Leadership does not involve holding on to the power of the people. It requires a building of networks and relationships based on truth and trust. The more the relationships stem from this intention, the less material-world contractual agreements are required. World peace can be achieved by simply agreeing that peace in the world is both important and achievable.

Once a level of understanding is achieved, the power of this understanding can be immense. The knowing that every person can contribute to peace on earth is a gift that any soul may hope to give and receive in a lifetime. Each individual does not require the permission of a leader, but rather a simple ignition of oneself in the hope that the leaders of the world will ignite this inspiration further.

Life Experiences

Each day the shaping of "who you are" is done through the perceptions of your own life experiences. All your experiences hold many roles with many players interconnected through the web of life. Sometimes the spider in the web may find itself in a spin, but your spirit will hang on with the knowingness that someone else will reach out and the light will be shining brighter from another angle in the web.

Never believe that your experience is alone. Never believe that no-one else has felt the hurt and pain that your soul goes through at times. It is this hurt and pain that allows you to see the love in others as well as in yourself. Your experiences cannot occur without anyone else in your life since you are all interconnected.

Through experience you will activate aspects of your soul's personality. You have the opportunity to rise above the challenges and to teach others of new learning ahead. If you decide to remain still in an attempt not to encounter hurt and pain, it will come to you through the natural course of life itself.

Many souls blind themselves to the possibilities of expanding "who they are" through the learning of other people's life experiences. You will often hear people say, "I have my own problems and I don't want to listen to that." That may be true, but the other person's struggles in life may provide you with answers to your own challenges.

Experience is not something that is measured by age, time, status or titles that are placed on you in the material world. Experiences are what you make of them and what you see as the greater purpose. Many focus on the end result whilst few focus on the growth throughout the journey itself.

Life can allow you to extend your love to people who you otherwise would not have invited into your existence. It allows the spider to decide if it wishes to poison those who come into its web or to invite them in for greater learning through compassion. By inviting and connecting with other souls you will see that experiences are interconnected at a much deeper level.

Within parts of the web of life, there will be areas of sensitivity and weakness but greater levels of light will shine through these voids. You have the opportunity to extend yourself further to others and join the energy together to form a bridge of harmony. Through this extension people have the opportunity to grow.

Whether experiences are seen as tragic or blissful, there are always moments that are deemed as polar opposite. It is this polarity that gives you the appreciation of the players involved and the greater growth and learning in it all. Embrace your current earthly life and attempt to see the happiness and gifts in each and every day.

Listening

Many speak of the word listening and often place its meaning on the outer. You may seek the whisper of a voice in the wind instead of the strong natural inner voice that lies dormant in each and every one of you. To listen to this voice you must trust that you are worthy of a voice and from this you will venture into the deep oceans of "who you are". A voice does not always mean it will be verbal, but rather a subtle connection inside of you that resonates on all levels.

It is often said that many people feel that others listen to their words but they are not heard. It is questionable as to what is required to be heard from the outer if the inner thoughts are of greater significance. Once one knows that their own thoughts and actions are of significance then the seeking of others to listen is of less importance.

The voice of the soul is one that expresses love, gratitude, joy and hope in ways that others less connected to their spirit may consider to be eccentric. It does not require a response or approval from other souls and simply accepts what is in front of them as truth. It does not discriminate between right or wrong. It may not know the difference between what is acceptable in a living physical society and what is not.

To be a voice for humanity is one that carries a greater level of responsibility. It requires a large level of patience in the understanding that the words expressed at this point in time may not resonate with the listener for many years. It may not be words that carry the message to the masses but rather expressions of confidence in "who they are" that spark the seeker to discover the full truth within themselves.

Listening in the physical world is greatly confused with verbal expressions from human beings. True listening is the silencing of the mind and allowing the soul to come forward with new inspirations and ideas beyond the limitations of the thought forms on the earth plane. It is the opening of the heart and mind to possibilities that otherwise would not have existed.

When one listens to their heart and mind, a flow of energy throughout the body can produce a euphoric feeling of truth. Lower levels of stress are experienced and the churning of the muscles in the stomach can cease preventing further worries from manifesting in the physical body. Both mental and physical health can be restored through a lighter attitude to life. This permission of inner trust and knowingness within you is the true meaning of listening.

Once you understand that you are worth listening to then you will discover that you will have more time and patience to listen to other souls around you. You do not need to be in a meditative state to achieve this inner peace but rather simply connected to your own spirit allowing you to be heard through your inspired living.

Inspirational living is the key to listening to yourself and others. By feeling the fear of someone in the room and replacing it with compassion, your presence can make them more comfortable in expressing "who they are" without judgement. This unspoken comfort is the greatest listening gift one soul can give to another. Allowing the inner voice to shine without words is a heartfelt expression that every soul is entitled to throughout its physical lifetime and thereafter.

Loneliness

When feelings of loneliness are experienced by the soul, an overwhelming sense of sadness can rush through the heart of the physical body, causing one to respond by disconnecting further from the people around you. Levels of anxiety never experienced before can be felt as you attempt to reconnect with other souls.

Being lonely is nothing to be ashamed of. In fact, it is healthy for the soul to spend time with itself in the hope that self-acceptance will eventuate. Solitude can allow the spirit to unravel the mechanics of "who you are". This self-discovery can be very powerful and exciting for some people, including those witnessing the cocoon unfolding.

Many people feel lonely in the presence of other souls. There may be feelings that no-one understands you. It is difficult for you to assume a lack of compassion from others when you are struggling to understand yourself. If you knew exactly "who you are" then the feelings of loneliness would not exist.

Loneliness only exists when the soul seeks love from others outside of itself. It is very natural for human beings to want to feel connected with other people. However, real connection with other souls occurs at a deeper spiritual level whereby the physical presence of other human beings is not required. Loneliness is an illusion initially created by the human mind.

The feelings that resonate through the mind when loneliness is present are that of self-doubt and lack of self-acceptance. You begin to question why people do not want to be around you or choose not to engage with you when they are physically there. A part of you may shut down with certain aspects of your personality beginning to fade away.

When in the presence of your own soul ask yourself what makes you happy in your free time. Ask yourself what you would do if this was your last day on earth. You would suddenly realise that people do love and care for you at a deeper non-physical level and you would make the effort to engage with them as well.

There are many souls constantly reaching out in their prayers at night sending healing energy and thoughts to those in need on the planet without ever physically knowing "who they are". There is a natural understanding amongst these souls that you will feel their presence and in your moments of doubt you will take in their light and allow yourself to shine.

Reach out to your loved ones in the spiritual realms and take the time to send healing energy to those who exist on the earth plane too. You will find that in time the feeling of being lonely will be more of a sweeping moment in your life rather than a constant battle of self-discovery.

Love

What does love mean? A lot of the music written on the earth plane is inspired by this emotion and feeling. Is love something that exists on one level or can it be felt on different levels depending on the purpose or the intention of the relationship? For something that cannot be scientifically measured, all humans know that it exists in some form or another.

Love is not something that can be anticipated or even planned in life. It is something that is activated from within a soul through self-love or the loving of others. The human brain cannot switch it off with logic and so this powerful emotion within the human consciousness can provide moments of euphoria or, in some cases, distress.

The polarity of love is no different to the polarity of the universe. To embrace the ultimate in life you need to be aware of the dark and light of all experiences. It is only through darkness that you can see the beauty of the reflections through the shadows of light. It is only through reflection that you are able to identify "who you are" and then embrace and love every part of yourself.

The polarity of the human emotion extends from fear to love. There is a lot of fear falling in love and then there is the fear of falling out of love. Being in love with another soul in a relationship is not always consistent. The only love that you will discover sureness in is your own self-love. You will never feel the fear of falling in and out of love with yourself.

If so much of the human race strives to find love, wouldn't it be easier to focus first on your own self-love? Loving others is a part of the natural process of connectivity, but loving yourself and your own soul consciousness is just as important. Without this love, you will never be able to understand why you embarked on this journey in life.

Once you understand and love "who you are", your soul will shine so bright that you will become an inspiration for others to love themselves. You will bring out aspects of personalities of those around you by making them feel comfortable in the presence of different people. It is this activation in other souls that is the greatest gift you can give through connectivity.

Connectivity and oneness of the universe is eternal. The magical tale of forever after is felt at a deeper soul level and no fear of separation is ever experienced. This is the love you should know and feel in your life. Through this love you and those around you will live a happier and healthier life.

Manifestation

In order to create a reality of happiness and love in your life, you need to believe you are worthy of those feelings. By putting your mind in a positive mode, you will be able to have an existence that is all-deserving of your being. Once you know and understand this simplicity of life, then your experiences will be filled with joy and laughter more often.

Ensuring that your thoughts are as pure as possible is a difficult task for most human beings. Living in an atmosphere surrounded by negative mindset and media can influence your ability to remain calm and relaxed about life. By observing tragedy and sadness in your society, you can also feel guilty for wanting a better life when others may be less fortunate than yourself.

There is no reason why you cannot assist others in the manifestation of a better reality. You do not need to confine your desires to your own physical existence. You can hope that other souls who live around you also share these wonderful experiences. Why limit the extending of your own light to those you are consciously aware of?

If you decide to place no judgements on the wishes you have for humanity then wonderful things can happen for others who are open enough to receive your requests. You do not need to provide them with matter that can be touched in physical form but rather feelings of compassion that will touch their hearts. They may not be aware this has been sent by you but will know on a deeper soul level they are not alone.

The more you extend yourself to others, the greater the discovery of "who you are". By understanding that your happiness and joy are a part of the greater consciousness, you can then empathise and create a better reality for those who are willing to experience it with you. If you are fortunate in wealth, take the time to dispose some of that wealth to those who will accept it with gratitude.

Every thought you create in your mind sends out a request to the universe. These requests are not judged by a greater human soul who decides what will or will not be delivered in your life. There are universal energetic laws that govern what is possible on the earth plane, which can then be influenced by karmic and life-contract blueprints. The outcome can be what is best for you at a soul-growth level rather than your physical world desires you wish to experience right here and now.

If you accept the possibility that life has a greater plan for all, then you can embrace "who you are" much easier than attempting to create a reality that was not pre-ordained. Manifesting the life you truly deserve is placing your hope and faith into your own soul that whatever is delivered to you in this life is for a reason. Attempting to sidetrack this purpose through constant negative thoughts will only create a bumpier road than necessary.

If you decide to trust in and surrender to your own being then life will begin to flow in a more favourable manner. What you may have considered to be a hindrance in the past can now be identified as an opportunity to grow and extend yourself. Manifesting a wonderful life is not just about creating physical world matter. It is the desire to discover "who you are" in this current existence with the hope that you return to the world of spirit with a more compassionate and loving soul through experience.

Meditation

If you wish to experience peace and harmony in your life, it is important that you take the time to relax and provide comfort to your mind, body and spirit. Meditation does not only involve stillness in your thoughts but also the opportunity for your body to move with ease and your spirit to extend itself gracefully. Embracing this purity within yourself and others allows you to grow through the discovery of "who you are".

If you are an active person who enjoys the outdoors, you can choose activities that involve this as part of your daily meditation. Taking a walk amongst the trees can rejuvenate you on many levels and even inspire your thoughts with different ways of thinking. The breathing in of fresh air opens your lungs and expands your mind so a clearer mindset can be achieved for the day.

Those who are less active and wish to stay indoors can create a comfortable setting in their own home or garden that suits their needs. Being aware of your surroundings allows you to cleanse the energy in your environment and become a part of your whole existence. The lighting of candles and burning of incense can purify the air and open your heart and mind to greater levels of possibilities and fulfilment.

True meditation is when you are able to focus your mind at any point in time to a mindset that is favourable for your experience. If you are feeling drained, stressed or depressed in a certain place, you always have the ability to see things differently if you believe that your thoughts create your reality. The environment around you is only physical with your mind having the opportunity to experience everything in life through spiritual eyes.

All experiences you have ever had in this life and cycles before it have been stored in your soul's consciousness, which exists within the mind. Your thoughts are not stored inside your brain and disposed of through physical death. The physical body does have memory, but no experience is ever lost from the mind. The ability to recall these of course is dependent upon physical limitations that exist through the human body and earthly experiences.

Your mind resides between the physical body and spirit body. There is a constant energy flow to and from the brain providing you with a reality whilst awake. When you are sleeping, you can experience dreams through an alternate existence in your spirit life. If you are greatly connected to your spirit body throughout your sleep state, the brain may not be able to recall what has happened in a non-physical environment.

Once you understand that the mind is not limited to the physical body, you can then attempt to focus on it through various states of consciousness. Projecting positive thoughts to yourself before sleeping will greatly affect your mindset in the dream state. By attending to your mind, body and spirit throughout the day, an alignment of energy allows a natural flow of thoughts to occur whilst conscious.

Conscious thoughts from your higher mind can be projected to your physical experiences if you are open and quiet enough to receive them. Your soul continues to experience and explore in the unconscious sleep state in the hope that new inspiration and ideas can flow into your mind throughout the day. Meditation is not about being quiet for part of the day but instead ready to receive guidance from your own spirit any time of the day.

Messages

Many people consider those of the higher vibrational realms to be the greatest and most truthful messengers of all. There seems to be a reliance on those souls residing in other spheres of life to provide insight and wisdom to those seeking guidance on the earth plane. But what many people do not consider is the power of their own soul in providing this guidance on a daily basis.

Each and every one of you has the power to guide and discover "who you are" within your current physical life. You have the ability to seek the deepest emotions and experiences that humanity can offer in the progression of your own soul. These insights can be witnessed through the teachings of those around you, including the wonders of the plants and animals that exist in your surrounding environment.

Messages come in many forms, from the evident delivery of information through physical sight and sound to a more subtle nature of feelings and emotions. Often people have the expectation that messages from other souls need to be given in a manner that is transferable to the earth plane's existence. When communicating between two worlds, often interpretation of this information is required due to the varying nature of life in these other realities.

The flow of life down a river or stream encounters many ups and downs as it progresses through the various stages of energetic forces. It is only when the life form eventually seeks the stillness of the body of water at the end that true silence can be heard. It is these moments of reflection on the journey up and down the stream that understanding of the path involved can then be embraced by all.

In the shorter moments of recovery as you are washed up against the rocks and attempting to seek balance, you will find the strength to rise again and take in the deepest of breaths to re-centre. This alignment of oneself is critical in ensuring that you will take another path that will lead your soul to its current life plan. This nurturing of your inner child from Mother Nature will fulfil your dreams and inspirations if you allow yourself to surrender and trust in the universe.

There are so many messages lost along the journey of life that one's soul chooses to ignore. There is always a constant seeking of guidance outside of "who you are" and a trust that another will inform you of "who you are". A true messenger will inspire and activate aspects of yourself that will provide you with insights that perhaps have remained dormant for many years.

Messages from loved ones and helpers in the spirit world can provide large amounts of healing along the path of progression. These messages are normally subtle in their approach, as universal law understands you are here of your own free will and choice. These souls hope to encourage you to self-love enough that you will trust in all that is given to you with a knowingness of gratitude in its delivery.

Many wonderful messages are provided to you all through souls that co-exist with you in the physical world. The speaking to another person with compassion and love can be a beautiful experience for all listening and encountering this natural energy exchange. Humans have continued to embrace each another throughout history under very tragic circumstances with such hope, faith and love to one another.

Any interaction you have with other souls that promotes unity and connectivity is a wonderful gift. Being a messenger of love and light does not need to carry a specific identity of an institution or organisation in order to be successful. Being "who you are" with self-love and love for others can be the greatest message you can give to yourself and your fellow human beings on earth.

Mind Over Matter

Many people believe that life on earth should be driven by the physical world needs and wants to satisfy the existence. Are you a product of your own life in a world of matter or is there mind over matter when creating your own reality? It is easy to fall victim to the circumstances around you. Attempt to see challenges as opportunities that can be overcome through the power of the mind and human spirit.

Each and every day people make decisions and choices without even consciously being aware of these. They decide what to drink, what to say and where they feel their lives should be. They may consciously make a choice to action something but this choice does not filter through the unconscious in the hope of its implementation into physical matter.

You must be aware of the universal laws of your own plane of existence and that of the spirit world. The earth plane is defined by time and space, and this serves a purpose to measure relativity in the progression of the human soul. Attempting to speed things up to satisfy your own needs may greatly affect others who are also a by-product of these creations. This can cause major imbalances in expectations.

If your intentions are to create something that stem from the belief that your thoughts will give you power and knowledge over others, it will be limited in many ways. You have already chosen your target audience, and have immediately disconnected from the possibilities of assisting others who can benefit from such creative energy. Those in the higher realms will have no interest in assisting in this cause as their world does not operate on a universal law of material self-gain.

The constant balance between giving and receiving needs to be addressed through the laws of matter confined to the earth plane. The energy flow of atoms bonding with one another works on the principle of likes attract like. This bonding of likeness is the key to the manifestation process since every creator needs a receiver. Acknowledging that the receiver may not even be aware of their needs at this stage involves complete trust and surrender in the universe.

Given that you live in a world confined by time and space, your thoughts may have the belief that if it does not happen in your own time then it will not happen. This impatience can cause you to unconsciously withdraw your creation request. The projection of your own thoughts has not yet had the chance to circulate and bond with other minds and requests of similar nature.

Part of your own current beliefs may not want your creation to go to a particular type of person, or even country, due to your own limiting thoughts of your audience. By thinking this way you automatically disconnect from the higher mind, the source of the universe that connects you all through no judgement. It is this connectivity, the power of oneness that links you to the source of all creation.

Open your hearts and minds to all living energy on the earth and universe. Allow yourself to be creative in many ways with the intention of wanting to give to another soul the gift of your creation. Create something that will not only allow you to be more compassionate but those receiving it as well. Also, identify the gifts given to you through the process of exchange.

Music

The vibrations of sound resonating through the mind, body and spirit can be a wonderful experience when you open yourself to this natural form of healing. The sounds affect your energy field to the extent where certain emotions and moods are witnessed by simply changing the pitch of the music. Softer and more soothing sounds give hope to the soul whilst more dramatic and deeper noises can leave the person feeling sad or depressed.

Music is a very large part of existence for the human mind in both the physical and spiritual worlds. It is extensively used in many realms for different forms of healing of the energetic body where the consciousness resides. Varying vibrations are attuned with precision to achieve certain results. Without music, many worlds would not understand the power of the human spirit in experiencing both compassion and inspiration.

The physical world generally does not consciously view music as an important healing mechanism. In entertainment, souls will naturally connect to one another through this universal non-spoken language. They will feel more comfortable in "who they are" when music is played in the presence of other people. In most cases when the music stops, people will feel less comfortable to dance in these moments of silence.

So why is music so powerful? Why does it heal so many both unconsciously and consciously? The answer is simple, it is vibration. Music is the projection of universal sounds that are in sync with one another causing harmony in the flow of energy. When harmony is achieved in the vibrations of sounds, a natural peace will resonate through the mind, body and spirit of those listening to it. Even people who are deaf and cannot hear the music will be able to feel the vibrations of this connectivity surrounding them.

Music in itself is a powerful example of connectivity and oneness of the universe. Whether or not the souls are playing the instruments themselves or listening to the music, when true harmony of sound occurs, it is irrelevant as to how and who delivers the synchronicity. All players are equal and there is the wanting of those creating the music to provide peace and inspiration to those listening to it.

When an orchestra of music is played, the listening and timing of others involved is of importance. One cannot be part of an orchestra with the mindset of individualism. There needs to be an understanding that an out-of-tune instrument will affect the whole outcome of the performance. There is a knowing within the soul that their small part is critical in the greater result, allowing their spirit to rise above their own human ego.

Thinking of oneself in an orchestra of life allows you to open your heart and mind to the gifts and wonders of souls around you. Only when you realise that your vibration affects the greater consciousness of life can magic truly happen. This realisation of being part of the whole is the key in the discovery of "who you are". Certain tones and moods in your life will project at different times depending on the compassion and love of those around you.

This realisation that your vibration, tones and moods can affect many souls including your own is the key to changing your life. If the current instrument you are playing is out of tune or not in sync then simply stop playing and begin to listen to your soul and those connected around you. You will feel through vibration what the best avenue is to progress which will allow you to express "who you are" on many levels.

Nature

The physical world environment that human beings reside within is perhaps one of the greatest wonders of the universe. The diversity of species of plants and animals is something to be embraced by all who seek comfort in their everyday lives. Knowing that you are not alone on the planet is important both within the human race as well as outside of it. Understanding and respecting this is of equal significance.

Most humans take for granted their natural surrounding environments. Some share the viewpoint that Mother Nature has the capability to recover from pollution, overuse of resourcing and destruction of certain species. A mentality that the environment is there to serve only humanity is something to be mindful of when raising children with earthly morals and values.

From an early age, the respect and gratitude for one's environment is critical. If a person does not believe their own living environment is worthy of love and attention, it is impossible for them to empathise with the connective environment that all living species reside within. Giving children the responsibility to care for their own living conditions provides a foundation in supporting the greater cycle of life.

By understanding that most living species share the same atmospheric conditions, a greater plan for all life can be considered. Thoughts and actions of an individual affects the greater outcome of the collective responses given by all. Once a person knows and accepts this, then changes in the thought processing pattern can occur.

If you are unable to place yourself in the shoes of either your own species or others then simply imagine yourself being impacted by your own actions. Once you consider this, your response begins with an individual self-gain motive in the hope that over time you will begin to understand your impact on the greater planet. This process of surrender can be a very rewarding and long-lasting journey for all involved.

As societies on the earth plane embrace and rely on the greater technology of man, there seems to be a further disconnection to the beauty of life itself. Happiness now stems more from the fact that the mainstream global servers are up and running instead of appreciating the rising sun in the mornings. If technology is down on a global scale, humanity may consider this to be as daunting as an eclipse of the sun itself.

What has been forgotten throughout the race to greater technology is the energy flow required to operate such intelligence. Energy used for all life on earth is provided by the earth itself. Technology cannot and never will replace the gifts of energy exchange that Mother Nature provides to all. It is important that this is understood to ensure that self-destruction of the planet on a global scale does not occur.

Can you remember the last time you had a spiritual experience with nature? When was the last time you walked on the grass, amongst the trees, swam in the ocean or admired the wonderful flowers without touching them? How much of your life is spent indoors in artificial conditions instead of embracing the nature of life in your surrounding environment?

If you find your life to be too stressful at times or just requiring some quiet moments, go to the places of nature that resonate within your heart. You will never hear Mother Nature complain or judge you based on previous experiences. It will embrace and love you as a mother does a child. This is the true nature of motherhood and every soul deserves to experience this unconditional love in their daily lives.

Negativity

When you engage in any thoughts or behaviour of a negative manner, you are affecting your own vibration of energy as well as those who surround you. Thinking poorly of yourself or others through lack of self-love or judgement is not healthy for your mind, body or spirit. Attempt to remain positive in your life as much as you can to ensure that your experiences are filled with peace and joy.

The earth plane can feel very smothering and dense when negative thought forms are projected into the atmosphere. Whether or not this is intentional is of irrelevance as other souls can pick them up in the confusion that it may be their own mind creating those thought patterns. This can create feelings of insecurity and uncertainty for those who are highly sensitive to vibrations.

If you are feeling sad or depressed, ask yourself if you have been subjected to thoughts or behaviour that are of a non-positive manner. If these have been created by your own mind and you are aware of this, attempt to seek methods of healing that will provide you with clarity of both the heart and mind. This can be in the form of modern medicine or alternative approaches of self-empowerment.

It is important to maintain a balance in your approach to positive thinking. If an event or circumstance has greatly affected your life, give yourself time to heal. Do not expect that if others progressed past this much quicker than you, that you need to do the same. Every soul is different, so therefore the reaction or response to a situation will vary considerably.

If you are subjecting yourself to continual mental or physical abuse, ask if you are deserving of this behaviour. No soul is so worthless that their mind, body or spirit is not permitted to experience love and truth. You are a powerful being with the ability to remove yourself from any situation or circumstance without harm to yourself or others.

Never allow anyone else to tell you that you are nothing. Do not allow your own mind to project thoughts of hurt and pain onto yourself or others. Seek the assistance of souls who specialise in areas of mental health as well as those who can simply provide you with care and compassion. There is always someone, somewhere who is willing to hear your thoughts.

Even though your life is unique, and different to someone else's, there will always be another person who can understand to the best of their ability "who you are". They will be able to accept you with minimal judgement and embrace those parts of you that are waiting to shine. You will find in, each other's company, that life can be challenging but also rewarding when souls come together and heal.

Do not hold on and treasure moments in the past to be the greatest that ever will be. There is always the possibility of something more fulfilling around the corner if you give yourself the permission to surrender. Open your hearts and minds to new experiences by attracting other souls into your life who will embrace you. Once you do this you will find that your energy will be much more positive, as will the environment you choose to live in.

Oneness

Does the word "oneness" mean that the joining of all souls together bonds the greater consciousness? Or does it mean that seeking of oneself is required first for this togetherness to occur? One cannot operate without the other, as the search for "who you are" is interdependent.

The only way to discover "who you are" is by activating certain aspects of your personality through interaction with other souls. You cannot see light without also embracing the dark. Only through the ignition of various sparks can fireworks of different shapes and sizes come together and provide a magic display of communal effort.

The self-discovery path for all individuals can be very enjoyable and rewarding if a greater viewpoint of one's life is observed. Once you understand that you cannot identify "who you are" without other souls and other souls cannot identify "who they are" without your soul, the power in this realisation can be truly transparent.

The term "oneness" means the opposite to separation. When you are not separate to yourself or others through lack of judgement, then connectivity of energy and soul consciousness occurs. This connectivity is the essence of all life in the universe including the expansion of further creation and understanding of "who you are". Your own identity is ever-changing within a dynamic universe.

Many believe that they will complete this physical lifetime existence on earth and find themselves "all-seeing and all-knowing" without the need to interact with souls who are of a lesser progression upon their transition to the spirit world. This level of understanding of how life works is very limiting and does not consider the many fixed and variable factors of universal laws that operate on a higher level.

If a soul has mastered many of the limiting factors of the human ego including judgement and self-gain, then why would they move on to another plane of existence and be concerned only with their progression? Individualism would defeat the purpose of mastering oneself to obtain greater connectivity and so assistance to souls requiring further teaching is inevitable.

It is only through self-reflection and feedback provided by other souls that you are able to learn more about yourself. It can take a number of players repeating the same message to you before you discover there is an area of your life that requires attention. Once you recognise this truth, even though it may bruise your ego in the short-term, it is hoped that the soul has enough hunger to move forward in the discovery of a new way of living.

It is important that the delivery of feedback to other souls is given with a caring and non-judgemental attitude. Attempt to place yourself in the shoes of those receiving the information and you will find a more empathetic and compassionate way to assist others on their path of progression. If the message is given with anger, fear and frustration then in most cases it will only cause further hurt and pain to all parties involved. This only results in further separation from the "oneness" of greater connectivity.

Outlook

Having a positive outlook in life can have a remarkable impact on your level of happiness throughout your journey. If you carry lower levels of stress and anxiety in the knowing that all will be provided for and attended to in some way or another, then circumstances can seem much easier for you. Some may view your life as being one with less challenges and obstacles than most, when in fact it can be completely the opposite.

Normally those with a very positive outlook on a day-to-day basis have perhaps had their share of the ups and downs of life on earth. They generally have a natural ability within "who they are" to move past old situations and see the greater purpose or learning in it all. They carry little anger and resentment towards themselves and others and have a strong faith that a greater plan is at hand for all souls.

Mindset is critical in creating your own reality. Often too much blame is placed on the outer in the hope that someone or something else will take control of the situation and direct it back on course. What is easily forgotten is that you are responsible for your own life and acknowledgement of this is very important in understanding your own outlook in life.

Taking responsibility for all your initial thoughts is the first stage in becoming aware of "who you are". Once you begin to consciously take note of the thoughts flowing in and out of your mind, you will be surprised how many of those thoughts are of polluting behaviour to your mind, body and spirit, and your environment.

If all creation begins with thought, then negative thoughts will only create a negative reality including the atmosphere they reside in. Cells within your physical body carry a form of memory that is triggered by a vibration of energy. Low-level thoughts of self-destruction and lack of self-worth only create illness within your mind and body. Your spirit then finds it difficult to inspire your path of action in life.

If you wish to be happy and healthy throughout your life, it is important that your outlook is maintained and nurtured at all times. If you find yourself feeling depressed, unmotivated, negative, nasty or judgemental, then attempt to address those thoughts and feelings immediately upon their arrival in your mind. Do not be afraid of them but simply try to counteract them with more positive thoughts.

Music is a very powerful source for lifting and enhancing the vibration and outlook of the human mind. It enables the mind to stop thinking for a period of time and gives your spirit the opportunity to come forward and express itself. If you can, play your favourite music frequently and allow your body to move in the essence of your own spirit.

Dancing by yourself or with others can provide you with moments of inner peace which then allow your outlook on life to be one of a more carefree nature. Do not be worried what others may think of you, as your spirit may in turn inspire theirs to take the leap of faith. Outlook on life can indeed be improved simply by observing your own thoughts and actions towards yourself and others.

Pain

When one speaks of pain, normally the first thought that comes into the mind is that of physical hurt inflicted on the human body. There seems to be a belief that a substance such as a painkiller can resolve most of this hurt. Physical pain of course can be managed through chemical substances, but what about emotional and mental pain?

It seems in today's society there is much focus on the administering of drugs to patients suffering any form of pain. These drugs can, over time, cause levels of dependency on the emotional and physical aspects of the mind and body. Regardless of whether these are given for mental or physical wellbeing, there needs to be a balance in other areas of one's life to ensure effective treatment.

When a soul is emotionally and mentally unwell, they will in most cases attempt to disconnect from those around them who are providing a loving and supportive environment. This disconnection is a warning sign that the person believes they are unworthy to be heard or even be present in the company of others. Further disconnection can cause more pain, resulting in possible infliction of hurt on oneself both emotionally and, at times, physically.

In many cases medication is required for pain and suffering, but it needs to be examined holistically. Hurt on any person living a human existence causes an imbalance in the alignment of the mind, body and spirit. If one is not healthy in the mind, this will in time affect their physical body and the recognition of their spirit in "who they are".

If the physical body is unwell and causing much pain and suffering to the person, this can reduce levels of motivation in everyday life, resulting in depression in some cases. It is important that the person is always aware of the imbalances between the mind, body and spirit and attempt to ignite one area of their life if another part is weakened.

If modern day medicine is required for the easing of physical and emotional pain, attempt to introduce alternative methods of healing as well that don't interact with the administered chemicals in the body. You may find that the body will respond to a range of methods working together. The pain can eventually be reduced or maintained enough to live a happy and sustainable life.

Be open and honest with your practitioners, and document and share how you are feeling on a regular basis. You may find over time that certain events, actions or times of the year affect your emotional and physical wellbeing. Cycles of varying seasons may affect you greatly, especially in the winter months where depression and physical aches and pains are experienced more.

If you are feeling emotional pain and suffering, speak honestly about your thoughts regardless of how irrational you may think they are. If a third-party neutral personality is required for you to do this, then do not be embarrassed to seek their services. On any occasion where your mind and body is hurting, feeding the soul can almost always create a soothing affect on your life.

Soul food can be provided in many ways as a comfort in your life. Playing music will almost always lift the mood, making you temporarily forget about your physical or emotional pain. Being amongst loving and kind company will raise the vibration of your energy field, creating a benchmark for further self-healing to occur.

Past

When you focus energy onto past experiences and memories, you will find this can leave you in extremities of emotions, from bliss to distress. Either way, you need to be mindful in the balance of your reflection time to ensure that you continue to live your current life on earth. Your soul consciousness will not lose these imprints left within your minds as they will always be part of you, now and in the future.

It seems that most of the population in the physical world spend a large amount of their time reminiscing over what was, or worrying about the future. Very little time is completely spent in the now, which is important in the self-discovery of "who you are". Temptations of shifting yourself into a comfort zone of familiarity are always attractive, especially for those fearful of seeking the ultimate truth.

The human mind is very powerful in filtering the truth of the past. It seems to be able to place itself into a screening mode that allows oneself to believe that the situation or circumstance was somewhat different. What is not considered is that the person viewing through the lens is not the same as the person at the time of the experience.

Perceptions of your reality will always change, depending on the time and space of observation. You are dynamic human beings with ever-changing aspects of "who you are". Varying levels of acceptance of these facets will greatly affect your viewpoint. Being able to observe and simply accept the truth without contamination is difficult for most human beings.

When many parties have been involved in a particular event in your life, the perception of this reality from all players will be achieved at different levels.

These levels will vary considerably, depending on belief systems, fears, past experiences and the intentions of those wishing to observe the event in the first place. Being mindful of these varying factors is important when seeking your truth.

You may find that someone who has taken a different path in your life returns at another point in time with new information. They may have since had other experiences that have opened them up to new possibilities which provided them with further insight into "who you are". Once they have embraced this new viewpoint, they may feel the need to share this with you.

Past relationships can be left with complex disappointments and expectations at the time of departure. High levels of frustration can be experienced, especially when one of the parties feel there has been an imbalance in the giving and receiving process. Bitterness can set into the personality as a form of defence, with possible future retaliation towards others resulting from these emotions.

It is important that you attempt to understand that hindsight can be powerful, and in most cases you would still have taken the same path, regardless of your current viewpoint. The reason for this is that the experience itself was necessary in activating certain aspects of "who you are". This has created the person you are today. Always try to embrace those experiences as a gift into the opening of your soul.

Peace

It is often said that peace comes from within; that it is something that can be achieved on an individual level without the assistance of those around you. To some extent there is truth in that statement, but for humanity as a whole peace is very much dependent on the state of minds of those around you.

The core of any human being is compassion, love and understanding for others. No matter how harsh life may be, human beings will always resonate towards helping others, even when they are in need. It is this reaching out, the wanting to provide peace and harmony to those around you that can affect your own inner peace in many ways.

If you were to spend your life meditating in a state of mind away from the problems of the earth plane, there would indeed be times throughout that in-depth meditation that you will come to terms with your own inner peace. You will attempt to escape the problems of society by focusing on yourself, but what you face within your own soul may be just as confronting as walking out of your front door.

Even if you are lucky enough to avoid all of this and raise your consciousness to a heightened level, you will be fully aware of the connectivity of the masses with serious global issues entering your mind. You will at some stage be aware of the pain and suffering of others and your soul will want to send love and light to those people in need. You can never escape your own inner peace or the peace of the earth's consciousness.

With the new-age growth in the awareness of connectivity, there needs to be a balance of peace within oneself and the peace of those around you. Once you acknowledge that you are part of something far greater than yourself, the earth will discover peace and harmony on a level that will shift mass consciousness. This is not achieved through mass meditation but rather through mass awareness in everyday life.

Through disaster, human beings are known to raise themselves above their normal everyday lives and dedicate "who they are" to assisting others. Thoughts of them not being good enough, or who should be in charge of whom barely arises, for there is no time for the ego to immerse itself in self-doubt. The power of compassion through the soul will burst through and simply work from the heart towards those in need.

Each and every day there is suffering on earth, with the masses focusing their attention when the global media bring forward the awareness. Other minds are responsible for providing awareness to you on what is required here on earth and when. These global minds can filter and dilute the information for political or economical agendas. Either way, if these global minds were truthful in the state of the earth, then global peace would be heightened.

Once a disaster has been sent through the media to the masses, underlying thoughts of fear and uselessness are sent to millions of souls. These souls will more than likely not send out positive and reassuring thoughts that all will be well, but rather feel their own vibration suppressed to the extent where they will no longer watch or read the news. They will shut down and send a vibration of fear and doubt to the souls in need, which does not assist the healing process at all. Not only is global peace now affected but also individual inner peace.

So what can you do in this situation? How can you restore your own inner peace in life and also assist in the restoration of the peace of others? All creation in the universe begins with thought. Try to project positive and loving thoughts to those in need as well as yourself. Visualise these souls in a restored state and thank them for the teaching they have provided to your own soul.

If you wish for your loved ones in the spirit world to rest in peace, then also send them positive and reassuring thoughts that all is well and together you will find peace throughout the process of grief. Once you start training your own mind to send peace, love and harmony to souls outside yourself, it will be much easier for you to start to send love to yourself as well, especially in your own times of need.

Possibilities

Throughout life, many possibilities and opportunities will arise. Some of these will not be recognised at all, whilst others will be accepted or rejected by you. The ability to identify what exists both within and around you is important when attempting to achieve a balance in your experiences. Once you know and embrace this, then life can become much simpler for you.

The key to identifying a possibility or an opportunity is to ask "who you are". If you are a person of high morals and values then you will naturally not pursue something that will leave you feeling guilty and unworthy after the fact. Being honest with yourself allows you to face the truth in any situation and see that not all possibilities or opportunities are suitable for your soul growth.

If there are times when you feel that your surrounding company expects certain actions from you, then go within your own self and ask what you would want from the situation? If the possibility or opportunity is to harm or inflict pain onto someone else, this will eventually only cause hurt to your own spirit once your conscience is aware of its own actions.

Through your own free will and choice, your awareness should always be taken into consideration when making decisions. If you feel that you are only seeing the impact of the choice on your own life, then perhaps you will face a forced reassessment at a later date based on the outcome on the other players. This can cause breakdowns in communication and relationships throughout your life.

By creating new possibilities and opportunities for yourself, you can inspire others to think in a more positive manner and become part of something greater. The development of new ideas and innovations requires assistance from more than one person, and in many instances can bring together a whole community.

Recognising that every soul has a purpose and gift can bring about further possibilities that otherwise may have been left unrecognised. The creation process within the universe is limitless, with all life connecting together through the interdependence of energy. This web of life brings about change in a dynamic way that allows you to unfold "who you are" through self-discovery.

Attempt to not immediately judge an opportunity based on its physical value. See the potential in the learning and soul growth that can be brought about through the interaction of others. If something does not feel right to you, then be true to yourself when making a decision. By expressing this openly and honestly, you may find others who think in a similar way, which can ultimately lead to a more favourable changed outcome.

One experience in life will be felt and viewed differently by every soul involved. By understanding that others need to be considered as well, you are expanding "who you are" through compassion and the understanding of people's needs. Placing yourself into the shoes of another is a powerful opportunity for you to see and experience the various possibilities in life.

You can sometimes place yourself into an experience momentarily to obtain a greater insight into the feelings of humanity at large. Taking this opportunity can then change the way you view all future possibilities that are presented to you in life. This does not cost you time or money but rather simple insight into the possibility that you are part of something far greater than yourself.

Power

The word power can imply a force of energy to implement certain thoughts into reality. This energy can also be given by others in the hope that strength, authority and leadership can be undertaken by another person. Judgements can be made through the expectations of those who give power to others to execute for themselves.

In a physical world society where structure and order are a part of its existence, power will be dispersed based on political and economic benchmarks. The need for order will bring about a sense of hope amongst the people that particular leaders will be fair in their resourcing of energy throughout the community. However, it is important that some level of ownership takes place by all who choose these figures of power.

When handing over your power to someone else, you need to be mindful of their intentions in using this power. If you are unsure of their underlying interests or motives, take the time to examine the trust and truth that you seek to align in the first place. If the results of your findings are either disappointing or unclear, then proceed with caution in the knowing that you hold the key to your own power.

A lot of resentment and anger occurs when someone feels powerless in their life, to the extent that no energy is left to execute their own thoughts and actions. They have allowed others to make decisions for them in the hope that the resulting outcome will be what they wished for. But no two souls are ever the same in thinking, so these expectations are unrealistic from the beginning.

If you feel that you wish to achieve certain goals or actions in life, then you need to take the necessary steps to make it happen. Do not rely on the energy or motivation of others to get you through the tasks at hand. All souls have their own paths in life and no individual soul will ever invest as much time and effort into your life than you. Handing over all of your power to others will achieve nothing but a powerless result.

Coming to terms with the fact that you are responsible for your life is the first step in acknowledgement of your own power. Understanding that free will and choice creates your reality provides you with a foundation of hope that you can always create a better life for yourself. If you feel that you have made mistakes in the past, take ownership of these and examine the greater learning at hand.

It is only through acknowledgement that you can then change your life. If you believe your existence is purely the result of others' actions, then nothing will change for you. You will continue to hold a mindset of hopelessness and victim mentality that produces further negative thoughts in your daily life. Embrace the knowing that you are responsible for your own life. This can then free your soul to the creative process.

So much fear occurs in life due to the resistance of one taking the responsibility for the power given at birth. You are a powerful soul waiting to discover "who you are". This can only be achieved when you consider the possibility that you are much more than physical matter. Do not wait until death to recognise this power. Take the necessary actions today to ignite the energy that resides in each and every one of you.

Prayer

Prayer is a form of healing that carries loving energy from one soul to another in the hope that peace and harmony is filtered into one's life. It can be done in many different ways but ultimately the intention of the thought is all that matters. If you wish for yourself or another to accept healing, then you only need to open your heart and mind with compassion and love.

If you find yourself placing judgements on the soul, attempt to work past these thoughts through positive affirmations. See them as light, and not physical form trying to work through struggles that exist through earthly experiences. By embracing another spirit and their circumstances, you are extending yourself on the discovery path of "who you are".

Prayer is not only limited to those in the physical world. The sending of healing energy to those who have moved onto various vibrations of life is just as important. The crossing over of a soul does not mean that the healing process is complete. Continuous healing on the other side will be necessary for most souls depending on their own awareness and type of passing into the spirit world.

Those who make transition into a world of non-physical matter may find the adjustments a little difficult at first. If they lived a life of attachment to strong material possession then they may still be drawn to the needs of the physical world rather than a new life in the spirit world. Encouraging them to move forward and let go of the past can be a part of their acceptance of a new way of living.

If you feel there has been unfinished business with a soul on this side of life or the other side, there is nothing preventing you in expressing this openly and honestly. This can simply be done by sending your thoughts to their spirit to process your forgiveness. Remember the forgiveness of oneself can be more difficult than the forgiving of another.

Sometimes you may discover that your mind is too busy to send clear and positive thoughts to someone. Another method of sending this healing is through writing it down. The flow of action that follows the words will provide you with a level of consistency and may reduce the opportunity for judgements or negative thoughts to enter the healing process.

Once you are done expressing these thoughts in writing, you can then choose to dispose of it in physical form as the mental energy has been sent. Lighting a candle can be very effective in reaching the vibration of another. All compassion and love sent to someone will be felt at a level that resonates with their own feelings.

If a soul is feeling sad or depressed, your prayer and healing can be felt much stronger than someone who is naturally vibrating at a higher frequency. This wonderful energy you send to them can shift their awareness in "who they are". It can also inspire them to seek healing from those who are willing to assist on the earth plane.

Purpose

The knowingness of one's purpose is simply the knowingness of oneself. A lack of understanding that your existence is simply purpose in itself creates blocks in the mind that can cause you to feel useless at times throughout your earthly existence. This negativity in thought patterns in an attempt to seek your life purpose can cause nothing but stress which has served no purpose at all.

By observing a person who has walked into a party-like atmosphere with a very relaxing attitude and no expectations of the event, you will learn that the person will experience the original intention of what the party was all about. The host of the party more than likely intended that people would gather in the hope that positive energy exchange would occur and new relationships be formed.

The person who has arrived at the party may not have intended for anything specific to occur but rather has felt the vibration of connectivity amongst those that are present. They may have walked about the room and introduced themselves to others in the hope that feelings of joy were experienced by embracing different souls.

Throughout the party, other souls may find themselves judging this person based on their open attitude to go with the flow. Blending with the flow of life enables the soul to meet new vibrations of energy amongst humanity, which can cause varying inspirations and interests that otherwise may not have been attracted or aligned.

As the relaxed soul blends and merges their energy amongst all walks of life, they may activate aspects of their own personality along the way. This exploration of oneself can be the beginning of opening a new channel of inspiration that allows the soul to meet a part of "who they are". It is this meeting of oneself that fulfils the soul's purpose.

The greatest purpose any soul can fulfil is the fulfilment of its own soul. From this fulfilment comes further inspiration and creativity that will inspire others to discover "who they are". These are the foundations to the connectivity and creativity of life, which is the essence of all existence throughout the universe.

Quality

It is often said that quality is of more importance than quantity. When attempting to design something for the first time, much effort is placed into the initial stages to ensure that the idea itself lasts throughout the various phases of the life cycle of production. The same also applies to your current life when hoping to obtain memorable experiences that will shape "who you are".

When someone passes into the spirit world, memories left behind can fade into the background and only come forward through reminders that are given on a daily basis. The most profound memories stem from times spent together that were well deserved, loved, adventurous, risky, filled with adversity and fun-loving and caring.

When your life is over on the earth plane, you will not carry with you the wonders of owning the large quantity of physical items you had whilst in your earthly existence. You will not be attached to the amount of money you had throughout your life. You will also no longer need to rely on the energy required for overeating, substance abuse and other indulgent experiences.

Life of the spirit is one that carries a drive in the knowing of "who you are" so that you can progress through the journey of self-discovery. When you are connecting to your soul on a deeper, less superficial manner, you will seek to find these moments in your life that seem to be so special. You will not take for granted the time you spent with yourself or others but rather embrace these encounters with gratitude.

There are quality gifts in the day to day of all living experiences. Despite being low on the financial side of life, a beautiful sunrise, a breeze through the trees and the sounds of birds singing can bring about richness in your life. There were times in your life perhaps when you did not notice the little things that surrounded you until the greater material objects were removed from your sight.

Seeing your reality unfold like a flower blossoming in the spring can be a wonderful experience for anyone willing to be patient enough to observe it. Observation of intricate details throughout the creation process gives you a sense of being a part of something far greater than yourself. It gives you a knowingness that you are never alone and time spent with yourself should be accepted with open arms.

You can spend a long lifetime on the earth plane and experience, observe or appreciate little that is around you. There are those who have shorter lives in the quantity of years but manage to embrace "who they are" and touch the hearts and minds of many people. Their exit service or funeral for their passing into the spirit world can be filled with wonderful stories of adventure, laughter and wisdom.

Regret

Many people frown upon themselves with shame of past actions and circumstances. They feel life could have been different if they had the knowledge or power that they currently have. What is forgotten is that your wisdom is the result of all your past experiences to date. Without growing through those events you would not be the person you are today.

Human beings spend so much energy lingering into the past or worrying about the future. There is an essence of fear in the air that previous lifestyle patterns will float onto the path ahead. This can cause you to believe that further contamination and pain will result, with your mindset projecting more doom and gloom.

Instead of seeing certain circumstances in your life as moments of regret, attempt to embrace them as stepping stones on the path to the evolution of your soul. The only way to get to know "who you are" is to see what you are not. Understanding that self-empowerment can only come when you are feeling powerless provides you with the realisation that you are a wonderful and worthy soul.

Every person has the right to live a joyful, loving and carefree life on earth. Your spirit is not something that understands control, rigidity and limits. It knows that the human experiences on the physical plane of existence will help you grow. Once you understand and embrace this concept, your life can become much easier, and filled less with regret and more with fulfilment.

Life was never meant to be a path of serious expectations. You should be able to see the beauty and humour in most of your past experiences. Ask yourself if you would follow that path again. On most occasions you would agree that those events shaped "who you are" today and you would not consider taking them away even if you had the choice to do so.

The human mind can hold on to something and be unwilling to change it even if it had a second chance. At the moment of complete surrender, you will feel powerless and unworthy of something better in exchange, and in this realisation you may take the old instead of the new for reasons of comfort. By removing these barriers, there are no longer excuses not to move forward in life.

Those who surround you in physical life can play an important part in how you view yourself and your past actions and experiences. Some of your regret can stem from the feelings of shame from genetic history, and the repeating of patterns that caused destruction of both self and the family unit. Expectations not to follow this path may have been placed onto you at an early age.

If you continue to tell yourself or others that you are not a particular person, your mindset can begin to undertake those actions unconsciously. It is important that you instead focus on "who you are" and embrace every aspect of yourself without attempting to project a personality that is not truly you. Love yourself enough so you can speak openly and honestly about your past in the hope that it will inspire others to live a more fulfilling and truthful life on their own course of self-discovery.

Relationships

Throughout your life, you will form many different relationships with friends, family, partners, work colleagues and people you meet along the path of self-discovery. These wonderful opportunities will assist you in developing aspects of "who you are" in the hope that you will exit this physical life with a greater understanding of yourself and humanity at large.

Some of the relationships you develop will be for shorter periods than others. As students and teachers to one another, you will have the opportunity to embrace a part of yourself that otherwise may have remained dormant in this life. Some people may bring forward anger and resentment in you to the extent where unfinished healing, either in this life or previous cycles of life, will rise to the surface.

These players who you may identify to be dark in nature can actually provide you with some of the greatest gifts that life can offer you. Your soul may have struggled with certain lessons of forgiveness, understanding, jealousy, resentment or trust. Once you recognise this through self-reflection and a willingness to be open and honest with "who you are", then you are able to free yourself of energy that may have been holding you back at a deeper soul-conscious level.

The constant struggles that occur between souls attempting to gain control and power over one another can provide a strong benchmark for understanding compromise and connectivity. Once you identify that life was never meant to be lived alone but rather in oneness, then further peace and harmony can be restored in your life.

Relationships that have been formed through family ties can carry a strong vibration of learning with the opportunity to expand "who you are". The parents who were genetically chosen for your incarnation have been selected for many reasons. Their living circumstances, personalities, belief systems, health and outlook in life can greatly influence your own perception of reality once entering the earth plane.

Your soul has the opportunity to accept and embrace what has been physically given in the hope that your spirit can rise above any impediment placed in front of it. Once you know and understand that your upbringing is part of your blueprint in life, you will be able to see the greater plan that has been chosen by you before incarnating onto the earth plane.

If you have been hurt by people you once considered to be close, ask yourself why it happened. Have you attracted the same types of personalities in your life before, resulting in similar outcomes? Did you overgive in your relationships, causing resentment? Were there issues of truth, trust or value that were not addressed and therefore not healed in past circumstances?

You will often find a pattern of behaviour in life through continuous learning of the same lesson. The players in the relationships will change but ultimately you will find that the common factor in these circumstances is you. Once you identify the key areas that are causing the issues, you can then alter your behaviour in the hope that you no longer attract those situations in your life.

It is important that you embrace all souls who enter your life and see the true gifts they have given to you. Do not waste the opportunities of soul growth on anger or resentment. Attempt to look for the reasons why they have come into your life. You have given them the opportunity to expand "who they are" in the hope that self-discovery will lead to a happier and more fulfilled life for all to enjoy.

Rest

True rest occurs when you allow yourself to relax in an atmosphere of inner peace and self-acceptance. It is when you are able to embrace that the now is more important than yesterday or tomorrow. You will understand that your mind, body and spirit require time to rejuvenate so a level of alignment is achieved that sustains a happy and healthy life.

When you are rested, you will notice that you are comfortable with the physical environment that surrounds you. The environment itself provides you with the mindset that all is well and you now have the permission to enjoy the time in the present. This place of rest does not need to be of material wealth but one of a quiet and respectful energetic nature for yourself and other occupants.

Being comfortable in "who you are" requires an ability to stop at certain points in time and embrace the real personality of your own mind. Seeing the humour and fun in life allows self-reflection to be more light-hearted. This enables you to see "who you are" in a much brighter way rather than through the eyes of self-criticism and constant doubt.

Engaging in activities that do not require lots of energy is helpful in obtaining a restful and relaxing state. By reading fictional romance or comedy, you are able to temporarily escape the harsher realities of life on the earth plane. You can witness the wonders of love and happiness without personal judgement of characters and outcomes. This can provide your heart and mind with further levels of inner peace and trust.

By participating in thought patterns of a positive but less exhausting nature, your subconscious mind will realise that these states of happiness create joy in your own life. It will then seek to find new ways in your current physical existence to maintain those levels of bliss. By witnessing behaviour in a non-fictional way, you are training your mind to accept these new possibilities in life.

It is also important that you do not subject your mind to negative, disconnected thought patterns. These can be driven by observing and hearing fictional or real-life events that involve fearful and violent behaviour. If you are feeling down about yourself, choose not to observe this type of media. You can decide not to turn on this entertainment and give your mind a rest for a period of time.

The company that you decide to engage with on a day-to-day basis can impact your ability to rest. If people are non-respectful of your personal space or values, this can cause feelings of resentment and hurt, only resulting in further unnecessary pain and heartache. Ensure that you are conscious of spending time alone as well as with others in the hope that a balanced nature will provide you with inner peace.

As you become more aware of "who you are", you will be mindful of your own energy. You will know when to slow down in your life and take the more scenic route throughout the journey. You will accept that others can overtake you on certain blind corners and bends but this change in direction is necessary as a part of your own growth and understanding. Observing is just as important as experiencing. Once you embrace this learning, your states of inner peace and trust will continue to grow.

Sadness

When you are feeling sadness in your heart, attempt to switch your focus onto times where you felt happy and rejoiced in your life. These moments of reflection can bring about a sense of ease that can carry you for a little longer. Try and engage in something that will energise your mind, body and spirit in such a way that you remember "who you are".

Emotions are a natural part of your existence and should be expressed openly and honestly. This does not mean that tears or physical fighting are required for recognition, it simply implies that your heart and mind should open to the possibility that someone else can listen and understand your needs. Once you talk about how you feel, you may find that a weight has lifted off your shoulders.

It is when you allow yourself to be carefree in thoughts that feelings of sadness can exit your heart and mind. By attempting to change past circumstances or control the future, you are actually limiting your reality to something that does not exist. The present is the time to focus your energy on rather than dwelling on feelings of guilt, fear or regret.

The past and future are untouchable by you as there are many souls apart from yourself who determine the outcome of the experience. No one soul is completely responsible for an event that occurs at a particular time and space. Many players have made choices along the way that brought about a situation at the exact moment of execution.

If you were able to freeze time in the hope of making different choices, you would find that the situation would never be exactly how you anticipated it to be. Someone else may respond to the matter differently, depending on the higher purpose of the interaction in the first place. The greater soul consciousness of the group is working in a manner that the lower human ego level may not be aware of.

Often a lot of sadness in one's life stems from the feeling of guilt and regret that something did not work out. It may be through the loss of a loved one, a breakdown in a relationship, financial security issues, poor health or a lack of self-acceptance in "who you are". Either way, you cannot always rely on the life force of souls outside of yourself to create a happy reality in your current existence.

Once you know and understand that every person in your current life is trying to evolve through experiences, you will see that on a deeper soul level the human race is attempting to evolve. Every person wishes to discover "who they are" on an unconscious level in the hope of finding inner peace, joy, love and happiness. Do not judge yourself or others too much throughout the challenging parts of the journey.

Life was not meant to be filled with adversity all the time. These moments will provide you with the opportunity to expand a part of yourself, but choosing to move on from this is just as important. If you are able to believe there is a greater plan in life, then you can at least attempt to see the light as well as the dark in all situations. This of course can take time. Try to embrace your current day in the hope that joy, happiness and love can continue to be a part of your life tomorrow.

Separation

When people speak of the term separation, they normally refer to being separate to someone or something outside of themselves. Very few souls have the realisation that being separate to yourself is of greater relevance in the assessment of separation to those around you. When you are disconnected from yourself it is known that you will separate from the love provided by those outside of you.

True connectivity of souls involves the recognition of "who you are" by all parties involved. If you project to someone a personality that is not of truth, you are creating a character that is separate to "who you are", resulting in the consumption of large amounts of energy. This facade will eventually leave you exhausted and disconnected from your own truth.

The further you project from the truth of "who you are", the more separated you will feel from yourself and society in general. This separation over time can produce feelings of isolation and paranoia, resulting in the manifestation of anger and resentment. You will believe that society no longer accepts this projection created by you, causing confusion in your own identity for you and to those observing you.

Erratic behaviour can begin once the identity of oneself has been greatly confused through wanting to please others. It is important that you recognise in these moments "who you are" even if it only involves a short glimpse into the light of your own soul. This small window of opportunity allows you to balance yourself once again in the hope that some level of self-reflection and self-healing will occur.

Feelings of separation and isolation are unpleasant for any soul experiencing these emotions. Deep states of depression can be witnessed by those observing such patterns, which may cause hesitation by others to step in and provide some guidance. The normal advice given to people is to seek out counselling or medication from professionals.

It seems that when humans observe an animal to be sad or depressed, they will take the animal and provide emotional comfort and love. They will not be shy to hug and kiss the animal and stroke it in the hope that it will come out of its state feeling joy and bliss once again in its life. Unspoken words are expressed with no need for complex discussions or reasoning behind the initial bouts of sadness.

Sometimes people don't want to sit and talk for hours at a time in an attempt to seek and find the root cause of their emotions. Perhaps the soul is not able to recognise what is causing the feelings of separation and depression but rather just wants to sit in company with other souls and experience the moment. This silencing amongst souls can be one of the most powerful ways to connect to other human beings.

Music is a wonderful way to reconnect souls with themselves and others. It is an unspoken language that all can feel and understand, without the complexities of having to know the source of the words or meaning behind it all. It is no different to the lack of verbal language between animals and humans that resonates. Connectivity is universal with separation only occurring when society creates barriers, boundaries and rules on how this contact needs to occur between souls.

Silence

The silencing of your thoughts does not mean they are of less value than speaking them aloud. The processing of information within your mind can involve different stages of acknowledgement, acceptance and understanding. The more you open yourself to express what you are thinking through preferred means of communication, then the greater your ability to embrace "who you are".

If you prefer to speak to someone verbally about a particular matter, then this of course is the way you feel most comfortable approaching them personally. You may decide to place your thoughts into writing in the hope that your emotions or theirs will not interfere with the intention of the communication. Others can opt to take the time to send healing and loving energy without the need to consciously express it in physical form.

There is no right or wrong way in communicating with another soul. If you treat someone else with respect, honesty and openness, the delivery of your information should be seen with the correct intention. Always ensure that you set out clearly what you wish to achieve in your mind before engaging in something that could cause further harm or damage.

The delivery of your message to someone else is just as important as the content. You can provide healing to yourself or another soul by attempting to listen to their perspective without judgement. Always try to take the approach that everyone sees things differently, and what may be considered the truth to one person may be misleading or misunderstood by another.

No soul would deliberately place themselves into feelings of hurt, anger, frustration or resentment if they had the choice to be happy. These underlying emotions stem from a misalignment of connectivity. Feelings of being rejected or not accepted can provide a foundation for difficulties which can ultimately lead to poor communication.

Being mindful of how a person prefers to communicate is respectful for the other soul. If they are shy and are not able to express themselves immediately, then perhaps an indirect method would be more suitable for them. If there are language barriers then perhaps you can use universal expressions that are understood by all. Either way, they will feel the intention that you are attempting to achieve through your body language and level of patience in understanding.

It is also important to understand how you communicate with yourself. If your mind is constantly busy and filled with negative thoughts, this is unhealthy for any soul's existence. Self-judgement or constant self-criticism can result in low levels of self-esteem and self-worth. Know and understand that you are a powerful human being with the right to live a happy and healthy life.

If you wish to believe this but currently do not think it, then begin to train your mind to silence the negative thoughts. Attempt to immediately replace them with more positive affirmations about yourself and others. Do not allow lower-level ego mental perceptions to cloud your happiness in life. Through meditation, prayer and continuous self-appraisal you can break through these thought patterns with persistence.

Once you know and understand that you are of light, then your heart and mind can be filled with the joy, happiness and love that words cannot express. You will no longer seek the approval of others who are outside of your own self, and there will be an embracing of souls in ways you never imagined before. The path of self-discovery will open much sooner in the hope that in this life you will activate further aspects of "who you are".

Simplicity

It is through the simple things in life that you can discover "who you are". Exploring the wonders of taste, touch and smell can bring forward memories of positive experiences into a reality that may seem hopeless to you at the present time. Embracing the moment as it comes does not require complex conscious thoughts or permission from others. It is simply there to be part of your existence.

When a soul moves into the spirit world, no material possessions can be taken. All that they ever created and experienced in physical form will remain in a world of matter. What is important is the growth and learning they encountered whilst engaging in a life that was surrounded by a complex world. Each and every thought on the earth plane affects the greater consciousness of the planet.

It is unfortunate that most souls making the transition to a new life on the other side will be unaware of the power of connectivity that existed whilst on the physical plane. They will view themselves as individuals struggling on a day-to-day basis attempting to overcome the obstacles of life. The existence of a higher consciousness will be a surprise for some and feelings of regret may become a realisation upon death.

Given that so much of the population is driving towards individualism, there is an expectation that the level of complexity in negative thoughts should be less. However, the human soul does not understand itself completely without connecting to the greater minds of others. It is through connectivity that simplicity can be achieved. Disconnection forms a complex selfish reality that serves no purpose at all.

If you disconnect yourself completely from society in an attempt to find simplicity, you will find that your thoughts can become more complicated. You will be naturally searching for new discoveries in "who you are" outside your own self, which can result in the creation of alter-egos and new personalities that do not exist in the physical world.

Maintaining a balance in your life is very important. The search for simplicity should not involve drastic, complex decision-making processes but rather the embracing of all that is within and around you. Attempt not to judge how others live but rather seeing the light in each other is important. The avoidance of others can lead to the denial of activating aspects of "who you are".

If you find the material world prevents you from breathing openly and honestly, then take the time to examine your current circumstances and make the necessary changes in your outlook. Objects of matter do not determine "who you are" at the soul level. They are simply transitory material possessions that are part of the set in the play of your physical life.

If you find that your stage is full of many possessions, there will be no room for new characters to enter your life. Judgements placed through material values can filter society out of your view. This can create a perception very different to reality. Attempt to share your material gain with others and allow every individual to shine their light onto your life stage.

Spirit

One's spirit is often a subject of discussion among souls seeking to attune themselves to the higher vibrations of life. This seeking by the soul is an attempt to fulfil itself on a deeper spiritual level that may not currently be felt in their life. It is something that cannot be experienced in words but rather an ignition of inspiration or passion to become a better person on many levels. The recognition of oneself can be a beautiful encounter for any soul willing to embrace "who they are".

Embracing yourself is not always an easy path. The struggle to come to terms with the many facets of your personality can be a conflicting and difficult process throughout your earthly life. Some souls may not accept parts of their own personality, which at times can lower their vibration through lack of self-love and self-worth. This in itself can bring about feelings of rejection and isolation which serves no purpose on their life journey experience.

Your spirit can naturally identify souls through the recognition of vibration which is the essence of life and the true fingerprint of "who you are". Your vibration is a wonderful unique identification within each and every one of you and should be felt much more often in the physical world. You may refer to this embracing as a gut instinct, an instant recognition of a person or the feeling of euphoria whilst in each other's presence. The blending of your energy fields can be a joyful experience for all of those involved.

There are many times when the spirit will encounter such experiences and quickly destroy those moments through earthly expectations and thoughts. You may feel this in the presence of the opposite sex and experience a level of guilt that you are not truthful to your earthly partner. Feelings of guilt or embarrassment can cause the initial natural connection to disconnect, which serves no purpose in the energy exchange.

It is acceptable to most of the living people on the earth plane that they can feel the loving energy of their deceased loved ones around them at any point in time. Whether or not this presence is from an ex-partner or family member in the spirit world, most of the time this is embraced with love and gratitude. But why is this presence not embraced in the physical world amongst other physical beings?

There is no difference with your spirit residing in the physical world or your spirit living in the spirit world. Spirit is spirit, so the embracing of each other's souls should be consistent across other planes of existence. Why wait until crossing over into the spirit world to change your thought processes instead of changing them in the physical world today?

Your spirit is immortal and has no limits of time or space, regardless of the plane of existence you reside in. If you live in a physical world that is restricted through the laws of physics, this does not mean that your soul or spirit is restricted in this way. Love does not understand limitations based on structure or form.

There are no limits to the number of souls your spirit can love. The interaction you have with one another should not be judged. A true soul-to-soul exchange is not based on the physical senses of touch but rather an exchange of joy that can fulfil one another on many levels. It is this fulfilment of the soul that allows your spirit to shine even further and embrace "who you are" as well as each other.

Stress

Whenever you are feeling uptight or not able to relax, look within yourself and ask if the source of this emotion is necessary. Most of the time there is no reason for you to react this way to life as certain thoughts and actions of others are out of your control. All you can do is maintain your own peace in the hope that others will join you on your more favourable path of living.

The mind can provide you with wonderful experiences of joy and happiness in your life. It is powerful enough to store these occasions in the form of memories which can be called upon at times of reflection or need. This empowerment can also be governed by your inner ability to over-analyse your thoughts and emotions to the extent where you can become confused and disoriented.

Often heightened levels of emotions can leave you feeling drained and exhausted afterwards. Regardless of the situation at hand, you can be feeling down for a period of time and not understand the link to the original source of the problem. It is sometimes easier to focus the blame onto others who may have contacted you and caused an upset in your energetic balance.

What is important for you to ask is why certain outside souls can cause you hurt and pain. Do they hold your power or approval of yourself or those close to you? Why is it that you cannot speak openly and honestly to them about how you feel and move on immediately after the situation? The delivery of these messages can be done with love and without the need to cause further hurt and pain.

A lot of stress that is caused in the mind is the result of attempting to change the past or worrying about the future. In both these instances, you have no control of the thoughts and actions of the parties involved and the eventual outcome. What you do have control over is your response to your own feelings and emotions right at the moment of the delivery of the situation or event.

Once you reflect on a particular circumstance, your own beliefs will immediately place filters onto the truth. You may decide at an unconscious level to only observe the negative of the situation regardless of whether or not the experience was very positive and loving. On the other hand, you may attempt to cover the truth in the hope that others will not observe what you have witnessed.

If you accept that life is a conglomeration of all thoughts and actions of those directly within your lives as well as the greater consciousness, then you will understand that attempting to control this would be impossible. Once you know and accept this, you can then lead a life that is fulfilled with the now. Observing the lives of others can be a great gift of teaching and healing if you allow yourself to know "who you are".

As you start to let go of control and begin to surrender, you will find that your life will become much less stressful. You will stop on the street and say hello to your fellow human beings and feel the love and joy of life and connectivity without wandering your mind onto the deeds of tomorrow. You may even be surprised to find that they have a gift for you too and the worries of tomorrow have been dealt with through the wisdom of today.

Surrender

Many souls who experience a life on the earth plane find it difficult to trust their inner guidance and the greater plan of life. There is a constant need to attempt to control the circumstances in a way that can inhibit the ability for new possibilities and opportunities to come your way. If you begin to open your hearts and minds to different avenues of thinking then your happiness can expand in ways you may never before have imagined.

Think of yourself as a ball of light along a string of many lights that are connected. Even though your intention may not be to shine "who you are" onto other people, it is inevitable that someone along the horizon will see your brightness from far away. You may inspire or provide joy unconsciously, which can leave you feeling appreciated without even knowing the reason why.

As other souls venture past you on their own journey in life, their lives may momentarily be lit in times that otherwise may have been darker. The sparkle that is felt as a result of your existence can leave someone feeling loved and not alone. This natural connectivity that occurs at a deeper soul level is the essence of all life. Once you know and understand this, you can then trust and surrender to the greater universe.

Sometimes it can take another outside of your own self to recognise your power and "who you are". Often when you are having a bad day, a person can walk up to you and provide you with a positive comment that can shift your mindset. They may even give you the answer you have been searching so long for. Some of you may call this a coincidence whilst others may believe it as a form of divine intervention.

Regardless of your current belief systems or knowledge of universal laws, all life understands that interdependence is required for existence. Human beings require the oxygen produced from trees whilst the trees absorb the carbon dioxide from humans to start the cycle of oxygen in the first place. There is an unconscious surrender that certain roles are played by different energies within the universe.

The same applies to your own life. If you attempt to control who or what is to play which role around you then this can result in an outcome not suited to your original intention. If, for instance, you believe that you can do a better job in creating oxygen than a tree, the result may be a polluting one if you are placing filters on the mixture of the air you decide to breathe in.

Your mindset needs to be open to the possibilities that other souls will be receptive to pick up your requests in life and execute them with an intention aligned to your own. Not everyone is out to target your experiences in a way that produces a negative result. If you think positive thoughts and trust in the forces of connectivity, then those on a similar vibration will be naturally attracted to your way of thinking.

The key to the attraction process is through lack of judgement. If you believe a person of a certain race, religion, gender, sex preference or physical appearance will be required to assist you, then you are limiting yourself to lower-level physical vibration thoughts which will not be beneficial to your own soul growth. Attempt to trust and surrender in the process of universal laws in the knowing that the right resources will be presented to you in the correct timing to achieve your intention.

Trust and Truth

Does the ability to completely trust stem from the knowing that the truth will reveal itself in good timing? Or is it truth and the knowledge of this that reveals that trust is required to surrender? Both trust and truth are very much dependent upon one another, with the more truthful ultimately being the most trustworthy people.

Many claim that their life is in a certain order due to the untruths of those around them. As a result of these untruths, one may state that they find it difficult to protect themselves from dishonesty and untrustworthy behaviour. But what is it that you are protecting yourself from? Is it your reliance on their trust and truth that gives energy to your own ability to trust and see truth in yourself?

A trustworthy and truthful soul can stand strong amongst the most corrupt extremist groups in the world without the requirement of others to give them approval. This approval is not needed for them to express their love for humanity as their inner being does not care about the mistrust and mistruths of the material world. These souls are above these vibrations and see the love and truth in most souls and circumstances.

You may ask whether or not there is a difference between trusting yourself and trusting those around you. There is no difference at all. If you find yourself having addictive personality traits and you combine your energies with like-minded souls, would overindulgence be the result of those around you or your own weaknesses not to trust yourself?

If you are truthful with yourself that you are responsible for the choices that you make in your own life, then perhaps you can start to trust in making your own decisions and not rely on the energy of those around you. Mistrust can only come about if you make the decision to place energy into another soul's hands and allow them to make decisions for you that result in disappointment.

If others do not directly make decisions for you through material world objects such as money, then perhaps you have handed your power over to them on a more personal energetic level. If what they speak of you is not true, then why does it hurt so much? Do you not trust in your own energetic projection of yourself to others and allow them to see "who you are"?

The more layers any soul places over themselves in the material world, the less trust and truth they will experience in their life. If they embrace "who they are" then surrender will occur naturally. This shining of the true soul will allow many aspects of their personality to be celebrated, resulting in greater happiness throughout their life.

Values

To value something in life requires an understanding of loss. It is normally through the removal of a particular object, circumstance or person that the true meaning of gratitude is felt. If a person cannot imagine what it would be like to live without something or someone then it would be difficult for them to place a value on what they have in the present moment.

The present is only a gift if you can see the value in life itself. To be able to breathe in the moment that you are currently experiencing enables the path of self-discovery to open in identifying "who you are". Attempt to take every day as it comes instead of trying to control it. By valuing the unexpected, you can then be fulfilled at a much greater level with peace, joy and love.

Self-value and self-love is just as important as providing compassion and kindness to others. If you do not respect "who you are" and seek constant approval of others, then expectations will result in further disappointment. You are the greatest investment in assessing and implementing the value of your own self. No other person, object or circumstance can effectively do this for your soul.

By valuing your life and identity based on material possessions, you will find that your emotional and mental states will fluctuate constantly. The imbalance of energy focused on the physical aspects of your experience can leave your mind and spirit in a depleted state. Self-awareness of your soul and self-education about different methods of thinking will not cost you any money at all.

Valuing the physical body that has been chosen for your current life experience is just as important. Understanding that your vessel is responsible for ensuring that your current existence is completed and fulfilled in this lifetime is something you should consider. By respecting that the body has limitations and should therefore not be pushed, your life can be more enjoyable through better health.

Sharing experiences with other people allows your life to become more valuable. Being a part of something far greater than yourself can place another meaning of gratitude through connectivity. The interaction of the soul with other life is a natural and significant aspect of human existence. By appreciating plants, animals and people, you are then able to value your own life.

Conflict can occur when people do not agree on the value of someone or something. It may be that they lack a level of understanding in other ways of life or are ignorant to the possibility that all human beings deserve happiness. Placing judgements on souls based on political or economic status, culture, race, religion, age, gender or sexuality only results in the creation of a valuation system in the mind.

A system of valuing someone based on categories or ranks of life can lead to further resentment, anger and fear throughout society. Leaders play an important role through the use of words when determining what the community should be focusing their energy on. If family ties, spirituality, health or education are not fostered then it becomes a challenge for those who wish to pursue this further within their own lives. Value yourself enough to express "who you are" in the hope that others will be inspired to do the same and follow your way of living.

Wisdom

Throughout your life you will be faced with many circumstances that will require some level of deeper decision making. Your response to the situation will be dependent upon your own judgements and perception of the reality you currently exist in. If you are open-minded, with a compassionate and positive outlook, the outcome should be more favourable for all involved.

The key to your ability in executing a wise decision in your life is the knowing of "who you are". Once you understand that you are responsible for your own choices based on free will then you are able to take ownership of the actions that follow the thought processes. If you do not like how you respond or react to someone or something, simply change your current mindset for a better result.

Greater experience in life does not guarantee more wisdom. The ability to see the bigger impact of choices made is dependent upon your viewpoint of the world. If the lens you are seeing through is foggy and clouded with judgement, then your perception can be very limited. Placing filters on the lens will provide a picture that is blurry with some people either missing or unidentified.

Being honest carries wisdom in itself. If you are able to face the truth in front of you, then clarity can be given at times when there is confusion felt by those around you. Often when uncertainty or mistrust arises in the community, people will attempt to seek the wise ones who they consider to be truthful. It is natural for human beings to seek comfort in someone they can trust.

There may be times throughout your life when you will not be able to provide wisdom to yourself or others. Emotional or mental challenges may contribute to a cracked lens and you may not be able to see the goodness in the picture at all. Attempt to seek assistance from those you consider to be open and honest with a level of compassion in their hearts who provide you with feelings of kindness and love.

Sharing positive information and knowledge with people around you can be a gift more valuable than physical-world objects. Your wisdom may not be accepted at the delivery time but later embraced when insight or understanding is required. Sometimes the person may not know what you are talking about until they have experienced a similar situation themselves.

A wise path does not need to be given to handle every possible outcome imaginable to the human experience. It is the intention and the tools used behind the execution of decisions that is of relevance. Handing over the recognition that everyone has the power and light within themselves can be a wonderful joy throughout your life. Knowing that you are a part of a universal force brings about connectivity.

Wisdom does not involve someone providing you with answers to your life. It comprises guidance and understanding of the greater reason for life. It allows you to respect and accept the energy exchange and embrace the gifts of existence. It knows that nothing is separate to "who you are" and each and every soul wishing to embark on a journey deserves the opportunity to be embraced and loved by all.

Youth

When you are youthful and carefree in life there seems to be no requirement to be on time or to act a certain way in specific places. This naivety towards the physical limitations of time and space is an indication that the soul is living its full experience through the human mind and body whilst on earth.

If you observe the way children interact with one another, you will often find that they enter into one another's personal space more often than adults. They do not seem to have the same level of understanding in regard to physical barriers. They will perhaps even share some of their toys with strangers in the hope to form new friendships.

As the youth grow into their skin and begin to conform to society they become aware of social structures and institutions. This can cloud their perspective on what is real, which can result in filters placed on their own truth. Their natural understanding of "who they are" can be replaced with who they should be according to the standards projected by those in their surrounding environment.

Allowing yourself the time to interact with children is important in remembering "who you are". Observing and mentoring them can also provide a foundation for believing in your own self and each other once again. Laughing out loud to your own jokes or humour can provide happiness to yourself and those who may be feeling a little down.

Always remember you are of spirit and the age of your physical life is of irrelevance. The cycle of life encourages the bringing together of children and the elderly in such a peaceful and natural manner. Both parties have fewer responsibilities of work and family, allowing them to release the seriousness that most of the middle-aged population experience daily.

The young have many ways of expressing "who they are" through creative means of thought processing. This includes drawing and painting colours and images that have an emotional foundation and meaning to their own experiences. They can express love for others in the form of gifts made with their own hands in the hope that this energy exchange will provide happiness.

Music is a wonderful way for the soul to become attuned again to its inner child. It allows your mind to be placed into a holding state where concepts of time and space are forbidden. The spirit has the chance to come forward and influence the feelings and emotions in the physical body. You may be inspired to dance to express yourself in more ways than one.

It is important that the youth within all human beings is kept as pure as possible. Regardless of the age of the physical body, everyone has the right to preserve their inner child that provides them with the permission to interact with themselves and others. It gives them a sense of connectivity and unity with other souls that is normally broken down over time through judgement.

Enjoy life through the wonders of embracing "who you are".

www.ingramcontent.com/pod-product-compliance
Lightning Source LLC
Chambersburg PA
CBHW051047160426
43193CB00010B/1088